# SERENITY WITHIN

## A Journey To Lasting Mental Peace

# DR. KURIAN NINAN

ISBN
Hardcase 979-8-89906-335-0
Paperback 979-8-89744-850-0

# Contents

# Acknowledgment

Writing this book has been an enlightening journey, one that has deepened my understanding of mental peace and harmony. It is with immense gratitude and appreciation that I acknowledge all those who have contributed to making this book a reality.

First and foremost, I extend my heartfelt gratitude to my beloved wife, Dhannya. Your unwavering support, encouragement, and belief in me have been my pillars of strength throughout this journey. You have always been my source of inspiration, and without your love and understanding, this book would not have been possible. Thank you for standing beside me through every step of this endeavor, reminding me of the importance of balance and inner peace in our own lives.

To my wonderful children, Aditya & Ryan, you both are the light of my life. Your innocence, curiosity, and boundless energy remind me every day of the beauty of the present moment. Watching you both grow has reinforced my belief that mental peace is something that should be nurtured from an early age. Your laughter, your questions, and even your challenges have inspired many of the thoughts that I have shared in this book. Thank you both for being my motivation and for bringing so much joy into my life.

To my dearest mother, I owe a debt of gratitude that words can hardly express. Your wisdom, patience, and guidance have shaped the person I am today. You have taught me the values of kindness, resilience, and inner strength. Through your life and struggles, I have learned that true peace comes from within, and this book is a reflection of those lessons. Thank you for always being my guiding light and for instilling in me the values that I cherish deeply.

I am also incredibly grateful to my brother and my close friends, who have been a constant source of motivation and encouragement. Your insightful conversations, shared experiences, and unwavering belief in my vision have played a significant role in shaping the ideas presented in this book. You have been my sounding board, my critics, and my cheerleaders, and for that, I am truly thankful. Each one of you has contributed in a unique way, and I deeply appreciate your presence in my life.

Beyond my immediate circle, I want to extend my heartfelt gratitude to the great leaders, thinkers, and writers who have explored the topic of mental peace and harmony. Their words, philosophies, and wisdom have been a guiding force, igniting my passion for understanding and promoting mental well-being. Whether it is the teachings of ancient philosophers, the insights of modern psychologists, or the profound writings of spiritual leaders, each of these voices has shaped my understanding of the subject. This book is, in many ways, a humble continuation of their efforts to spread awareness about the importance of mental well-being.

My inspiration to write this book also stems from witnessing the struggles of young adults and working professionals who navigate the relentless stress of daily life. In today's fast-paced world, the pressure to meet expectations, achieve success, and maintain personal responsibilities often leads to an overwhelming sense of anxiety and burnout. I have seen firsthand how these challenges affect mental health, relationships, and overall well-being. This book is dedicated to all those individuals who are seeking a path toward peace and balance amidst their demanding lives. If my words can bring even the slightest change in their outlook, help them pause and reflect, or encourage them to prioritize their mental health, I will consider this endeavor a success.

I am a firm believer that just as we take care of our physical health through exercise, be it cardio, weightlifting, or any other form of physical activity, we must also exercise our minds. Mental well-being is not something that happens by chance; it requires conscious effort, practice, and dedication. The practices and insights shared in this book are designed to serve as a form of mental exercise, enabling individuals to cultivate resilience, mindfulness, and inner harmony. My hope is that readers will incorporate these principles into their daily lives and experience the transformative power of a peaceful mind.

Lastly, I would like to express my sincere appreciation for the advancements in technology, particularly artificial intelligence tools, which have played a crucial role in bringing this book to life. AI has provided me with resources, research, and organizational tools that have made the writing process smoother and more efficient. From gathering information to structuring ideas, these technological innovations have been instrumental in making my vision a reality. I am truly grateful for the opportunities that these tools have provided me to enhance the depth and clarity of my work.

As I conclude this acknowledgment, I want to emphasize that this book is not just a collection of words; it is a reflection of my thoughts, experiences, and aspirations for a world where mental peace and harmony are prioritized. I sincerely hope that every reader finds something valuable within these pages—whether it be a newfound perspective, a practical tool, or simply a moment of tranquility amidst the chaos of daily life.

To everyone who has been a part of this journey, whether directly or indirectly, thank you. Your support, wisdom and encouragement have made this book possible, and I am forever grateful.

# CHAPTER 1

# Understanding Mental Peace: A Journey to Inner Calm

We've all been there—spinning through life like a stressed-out circus performer, juggling deadlines, family drama, and a to-do list that somehow grows faster than we can check things off. Just when we think we're catching up, boom—another email, another chore, another unexpected existential crisis (thanks, overthinking!). Every now and then, we all dream of escaping to a quiet, peaceful paradise—maybe a remote beach, a mountain retreat, or even just five uninterrupted minutes in the bathroom. But what exactly is this mystical thing called "mental peace," and why does it seem harder to find than a sock that vanished in the laundry? Let's unravel this mystery, figure out why inner calm feels so elusive, and, most importantly, how we can actually get some!

What is Mental Peace?

Imagine sitting by a calm lake on a lazy Sunday afternoon, the water perfectly still, and the only sound you hear is the rustling of leaves. You're completely at peace with the world. No emails to check. No traffic to navigate. No worries about your next big presentation. You're just… present.

That, my friend, is the essence of mental peace. It's not about avoiding challenges or living in a bubble of relaxation. Mental peace is about having an inner sense of calm that doesn't get shaken by the world around you. It's an internal state where you feel grounded, balanced, and capable of handling life's ups and downs without feeling overwhelmed.

Let me tell you about my friend Rachel—aka the ultimate overachiever—who came to me looking like she had just run a marathon through a hurricane. A marketing powerhouse in her 30s, Rachel had everything society tells us we need to be happy: a high-flying career, a shiny collection of promotions, a gorgeous apartment with a view (the kind that makes people jealous on Instagram), and enough travel stamps in her passport to make a flight attendant envious.

And yet—she was miserable.

Rachel wasn't just tired; she was exhausted down to her soul. She felt like a hamster on a wheel, sprinting at full speed but going absolutely nowhere. No matter how many milestones she hit, how many LinkedIn congratulations she received, or how many dreamy vacations she booked, something always felt off—like she was chasing a finish line that kept moving further away.

One night, over coffee (and an emergency slice of cake), she finally admitted, "I don't even know why I'm doing all of this anymore." She had spent so long checking the boxes of success that she had forgotten to ask herself if those boxes even mattered. Her happiness was tied to external trophies—job titles, designer handbags, fancy dinners—but inside, she felt like a beautifully wrapped gift box that was completely empty.

That's when we flipped the script. Instead of strategizing for her next career leap, we started strategizing for her sanity. We talked about mindfulness, relaxation, and— gasp! —the idea of slowing down. At first, the concept of sitting still without plotting her next move felt as unnatural as eating soup with a fork. But little by little, she started shifting her focus inward. She swapped late-night emails for moments of silence, traded achievement-chasing for presence, and—most importantly—allowed herself to breathe without the pressure of "What's next?"

And guess what? She found it.

Not in a title, a paycheck, or an exotic getaway—but in herself. Rachel learned that happiness isn't about running toward something; it's about being at peace right where you are. And when she finally stopped sprinting through life like it was an obstacle course, she realized she had everything she needed all along.

Now, you might be wondering: isn't mental peace just a fancy way of talking about relaxation or happiness? Not quite. While relaxation and happiness are important, they are often temporary. You can feel relaxed after a yoga class or happy after a good meal at P.F. Chang's, but those feelings fade once you leave the class or finish eating. Mental peace, however, sticks around—it's a way of being that transcends temporary experiences. It's the foundation that makes those fleeting moments of joy possible.

## The Connection Between Mental Peace and Happiness

So, how does mental peace connect to happiness? Well, here's the deal: when we're mentally at peace, we don't depend on external circumstances to make us feel happy. Let's face it—happiness that's based on things, achievements, or the approval of others is fleeting at best. Sure, you might feel elated after buying that new Mercedes or landing that promotion, but that excitement fades. You're left seeking the next big thing to fill that void.

Let's take Thomas – a man who seemed to have it all. A senior manager at a high-flying tech company with a salary that could make even the richest billionaire raise an eyebrow. He had the job, the title, and the car that made the neighbors whisper with envy – yet he was a walking stress ball.

Let me set the scene: Thomas would walk into work every morning, looking like he'd just time-traveled out of a dystopian movie. The only thing missing was a neon sign above his head flashing "HELP ME!" He was the picture-perfect example of what we all think success should look like – a polished, high-powered manager who'd made it to the top, but at the price of his sanity.

And let's not forget his home life. You know that feeling when you're so burned out you can't even look at a pizza without wanting to cry? That was Thomas. He came home every day, staring blankly at his front door as if it were the entrance to a black hole. He had zero time, zero energy, and zero interest in spending time with his family, let alone his friends. They probably wondered if he had a second job as a ghost because he was always *there* but never really *present*.

Now, here's where it gets dramatic. One day, during one of our friendly chats (which, let's be real, started out as him unloading his complaints about his endless emails), Thomas had an epiphany. It was like a lightbulb turned on, except that the lightbulb had a few existential questions attached to it. "Maybe… just maybe… my happiness isn't tied to my paycheck?" He looked at me with wide eyes, as if he had just discovered the meaning of life.

It turns out that Thomas had been chasing the ever-elusive "happiness" that comes with external validation – you know, the kind where you think a promotion will fix everything. But in reality, that shiny promotion was just a ticket to *more* stress and *less* joy. Oops. So, he made the brilliant decision to stop playing life's game with the wrong strategy. Who needs more stress, right?

Cue dramatic music: Thomas went on a journey of self-discovery that would make even the most seasoned meditators blush. I helped him carve out some boundaries at work (you know, like the kind that says, "No, I am *not* answering that email at 9 PM"). We worked on cultivating habits of self-care, which, let's be honest, started with convincing him that *sleeping* wasn't overrated. And then, we dabbled in gratitude – not the kind where you're like, "Oh, I'm thankful for my comfy couch," but more like, "Hey, I'm grateful that I don't need to check my emails every five minutes."

Slowly but surely, Thomas started to shed that anxious, stressed-out version of himself like an old, worn-out sweater. He began to feel *less* like a hamster on a never-ending treadmill and more like a human being who could actually breathe. As his mental peace grew, so did his ability to find real happiness. And it wasn't in a paycheck, a promotion, or a shiny new tech gadget (although those are fun). It was in the little moments – the peaceful evenings, the quiet mornings, and the fact that he could actually remember what his family looked like without squinting.

Moral of the story? Happiness isn't something you can buy or achieve on someone else's terms. It's something you find within – after you've taken a deep breath, set some boundaries, and stopped letting your email inbox dictate your life. Oh, and it's also important to remember that sometimes the best way to find peace is to take a step back from your shiny career and say, "You know what? I'm good. I deserve to be happy *right now*."

When we cultivate mental peace, we begin to realize that true happiness isn't found in external sources of validation or material success. It comes from within, from a deep sense of acceptance, contentment, and calm. And when we operate from a place of peace, the happiness we experience lasts much longer than the fleeting kind that comes from things or achievements.

## Common Obstacles to Mental Peace

As much as we'd like to maintain a state of mental peace, it's not always easy. Life is full of distractions, challenges, and stresses that can pull us out of our calm. Let's take a look at some common obstacles to mental peace and how they affect us.

## 1. Stress

Stress is probably the number one enemy of mental peace. We all know that feeling—your mind racing, your heart pounding, your body tense as you try to keep up with the demands of life. Whether it's work deadlines, financial pressures, or personal struggles, stress seems to be a constant companion for many of us.

My very good friend Annie's life was like a hamster on a wheel, but instead of a hamster, it was her—stressfully running, spinning, and somehow always feeling like she wasn't getting anywhere. If there was a way to create a to-do list for her to-do lists, Annie would have done it. But no matter how many checkboxes she ticked off, she felt like there was always another mountain of tasks waiting to be conquered.

One afternoon, she sat across from me, looking like she'd just survived a tornado. "I just don't get it," she said, dramatically running a hand through her hair. "I'm juggling a hundred things at work, I have friends sending me invitations to things I can't remember agreeing to, and I'm pretty sure I forgot to feed my plants for a week. Everything feels like it's crashing down."

I nodded sympathetically. "Sounds stressful."

She gave me a look like I'd just pointed out that the sky was blue. "No kidding, Sherlock," she replied. "I'm literally living in a pressure cooker, and I'm the roast chicken."

So, I decided I wanted to get things right for her. First, I asked her what she did to relax. Annie stared at me as if I had asked her if she could juggle flaming swords. "Relax? Do you mean when I'm asleep? Because that's pretty much the only time I'm not panicking about something."

I realized it was time for an intervention. We needed to make a plan for *real* relaxation. And no, it didn't involve her sitting in front of Netflix binge-watching three seasons of a show she'd already seen, just to numb the stress. (As tempting as that might sound.)

We started with something simple: breathing exercises. "Breathe in for four seconds, hold for four seconds, and breathe out for four seconds," I said.

She blinked at me as if I had suggested she meditate on a mountaintop in Tibet. "That sounds like something you read on a Pinterest board," she said.

But desperate times called for desperate measures, so Annie gave it a try. She started with a five-minute session. The first two minutes were spent wondering if she'd left her phone on silent, the next two minutes were spent mentally rearranging her closet in her head, and by the fifth minute, she had forgotten she was supposed to be relaxing. But slowly, very slowly, it started to click.

One Saturday, when Annie was about to launch into full-on stress mode about a work project. Instead of running around like a chicken with its head cut off, she took five minutes. Just five. She closed her eyes, did her breathing exercises, and resisted the urge to check her email every five seconds. When she opened her eyes, she was shocked to find that she felt... *a little bit calmer.* It was like someone had taken a weight off her shoulders without her having to carry it herself.

Now, Annie still had her moments (I mean, who doesn't?). But she learned how to recognize when her stress level was rising and take a breather before it turned into a full-blown meltdown. She's even started telling her friends, "Sorry, I can't make it. I need a mental health day!" And for the first time, she wasn't ashamed of it.

Her stress was still there, but it wasn't running her life anymore. And let's be honest, when Annie gets too stressed now, we just remind her: "Breathe, girl. It's like you're on a bicycle, and the only way to make it stop is to *slow down.*" And if that doesn't work, she knows she can always feed her plants—after all, they're pretty low maintenance compared to her work emails.

## 2. Overthinking

Overthinking is another major roadblock to mental peace. We've all been there, right? Sitting up late at night, replaying a conversation in your head, wondering if you said the wrong thing, or worrying about something that might happen in the future. Our minds can sometimes be our own worst enemy, making us overanalyze and overthink every little detail.

Sarah was a classic overthinker. You know the type: the one who can spend hours deciding what to eat for dinner, only to end up with a bowl of cereal because, well, it was "easier." But Sarah's overthinking wasn't just confined to her meals; it seeped into her work life, her friendships, and pretty much every other aspect of her existence.

One day, Sarah came to me looking like she'd just run a marathon—mentally, not physically. She had a big presentation at work, and it had her in knots. "What if I say the wrong thing? What if my slides are terrible? What if my boss's dog barks in the middle of my presentation and I completely lose my audience?" Yes, she was worried about her boss's dog, too.

It turned out that Sarah was constantly replaying scenarios in her head. She'd spend an hour trying to figure out if she'd made the right comment in a meeting, or worse—

wondering if her colleague's 'good morning' was actually a thinly veiled criticism. Classic Sarah.

So, we started working on calming her mental hamster wheel. First, we introduced the concept of mindfulness, which, at first, Sarah found hilarious. "So, you're saying I should just *be* present? Like, not think about anything? At all?" Yep, exactly. Eventually, she agreed to give it a try.

The breakthrough moment came when Sarah was at a friend's birthday party. She'd spent the whole day overthinking what to wear, what to say, and whether or not it was socially acceptable to eat three slices of cake. (Spoiler alert: It was.) Instead of obsessing over every little detail, she just decided to show up and enjoy herself. And guess what? She did! Not only did she have a blast, but she didn't spend the whole evening analyzing every word she said or wondering if people noticed her cake-induced sugar high.

After that, Sarah started to let go of her overthinking habits bit by bit. And while she still couldn't decide whether to order Thai food or sushi on a Friday night without a 30-minute internal debate, she was getting better at focusing on the present and leaving her stress (and overanalysis) behind.

Now, Sarah still jokes about how much time she used to waste stressing over every tiny detail. But instead of letting it overwhelm her, she learned to laugh at herself—and that, my friend, was the start of her mental peace.

## 3. Societal Pressures

There's no escaping it: we live in a world where societal expectations are often at odds with our personal needs and desires. Whether it's the pressure to have a certain job, live a particular lifestyle, or meet certain beauty standards, these external pressures can create internal conflict and rob us of our peace.

My nephew was feeling torn between following his true passions and meeting the expectations of his family. My brother had always encouraged him to pursue a "practical" career, but my nephew loved journaling and wanted to build a life around it. The pressure he felt was making him anxious and unhappy.

With the right advice, he learned to embrace his true calling and stop worrying about what others thought of him. He realized that mental peace came from accepting himself for who he truly was and not living according to others' expectations. By doing so, he began to feel a sense of freedom and joy he hadn't experienced in years.

## The Path Forward

Achieving mental peace isn't about escaping life's challenges—it's about learning how to handle them with grace and calm. By recognizing the connection between mental peace and happiness, we can shift our focus from external sources of validation to nurturing our inner calm. And while there will always be obstacles—stress, overthinking, and societal pressures—there are ways to overcome them and find lasting peace. Just like Thomas, Annie, Sarah, and my nephew, we all have the ability to choose peace, one moment at a time. And once we do, we'll find that happiness follows naturally.

# CHAPTER 2

# Understanding Mindfulness and Meditation Practices: The Path to Inner Peace

Alright, let's talk about something that's gaining a lot of attention lately: mindfulness and meditation. It sounds trendy, right? But in reality, these practices are ancient and incredibly powerful tools for transforming your mind, body, and overall well-being. You don't need to be a monk or a guru to benefit from mindfulness or meditation—you can incorporate these practices into your life, no matter how busy or chaotic it feels. So, let's explore why mindfulness and meditation are essential and how they can change your mental health for the better.

What is Mindfulness?

Mindfulness is simply the art of being present. It's about paying attention to the current moment, fully aware of your thoughts, feelings, and surroundings without judgment. It's the opposite of letting your mind wander aimlessly to the past or the future. Instead of getting lost in worries or distractions, mindfulness helps you center yourself in the "here and now."

Think of it like this: Have you ever been so wrapped up in your thoughts that you missed out on what's actually happening around you? Maybe you're eating a meal, but you're not really tasting it because you're thinking about your to-do list. Mindfulness brings you back to that meal—making it more enjoyable, more meaningful, and far less stressful.

**The Role of Meditation in Cultivating Mindfulness**

Meditation is the practice that helps you develop mindfulness. It's like the gym for your mind. Just like how you exercise your body to build strength, you use meditation to strengthen your ability to focus, observe your thoughts, and remain calm under pressure. Meditation isn't about stopping your thoughts; it's about watching them without getting caught up in them. When you meditate regularly, you begin to cultivate a deeper sense of awareness, peace, and balance in your daily life.

You don't have to meditate for hours on end to feel the benefits. Even 5–10 minutes of focused breathing and observation can work wonders in calming your mind, improving focus, and reducing stress.

A Timeless Example: Buddha's Enlightenment and the Power of Meditation

One of the most profound stories about the power of mindfulness and meditation comes from Buddha's path to enlightenment. Before he became the Buddha, Siddhartha Gautama was a prince who left his luxurious life behind in search of the truth about life, suffering, and peace. After years of extreme practices and studying with various teachers, he realized that the key to true peace lay not in self-denial or indulgence, but in a balanced approach—what we now call the Middle Way.

Siddhartha decided to meditate under a Bodhi tree, vowing to stay there until he found the answers he sought. As he sat in deep meditation, distractions began to arise. Temptations, doubts, and fear surfaced, and Mara, the demon of desire and illusion, tried to sway him from his path. Mara sent waves of fear, lust, and distractions to disturb Siddhartha's focus. But Siddhartha, through mindfulness, simply observed these disturbances without reacting. He didn't allow them to control him. Instead, he let them come and go, like clouds drifting across the sky.

Through this mindfulness, Siddhartha went deeper into his meditation, becoming more aware of the impermanence of his thoughts and emotions. Finally, after a period of intense focus and stillness, Siddhartha achieved enlightenment. He understood the nature of suffering and the path to liberation—insights that became the Four Noble Truths and the foundation of Buddhism.

This story portrays that mindfulness and meditation helped Buddha transcend the distractions of the mind and see things clearly. His practice of non-attachment— observing thoughts and feelings without getting caught up in them—led to profound mental clarity and inner peace.

## The Science Behind Mindfulness and Meditation

You might be wondering—what happens inside the brain when we practice mindfulness and meditation? Well, studies show that these practices have a powerful impact on the brain's structure and function. Regular meditation can increase gray matter in areas of the brain associated with memory, emotional regulation, and self-awareness. It can also help reduce the size of the amygdala, the part of the brain that controls fear and stress responses.

For example, a Harvard study found that just 8 weeks of mindfulness meditation increased gray matter in the hippocampus, the area of the brain associated with memory and learning. At the same time, it reduced the size of the amygdala, the part of the brain responsible for fear and stress responses. This means that regular meditation can help you become more focused, emotionally resilient, and less reactive to stress.

Another study published in *JAMA Internal Medicine* found that mindfulness meditation can be as effective as antidepressants in reducing symptoms of anxiety and depression. And if that's not enough, meditation has also been shown to lower blood pressure, improve sleep quality, and even boost immune function. So, while mindfulness and meditation might seem like "soft" practices, their impact on your brain and body is anything but.

Teachings from ancient texts and traditions on the power of meditation:

Meditation has been practiced for thousands of years, and ancient wisdom on the subject is rich and diverse, spanning many cultures and spiritual traditions. Here are a few key teachings from ancient texts and traditions that shed light on the power of meditation:

1. Buddhist Wisdom:

- Mindfulness as the Path to Liberation (Dhammapada): One of the central teachings in Buddhism is the practice of mindfulness, which is closely tied to meditation. In the *Dhammapada*, Buddha said, "You are what you think. All that you are arises from your thoughts. With your thoughts, you make your world." This emphasizes the power of the mind and how meditation helps in calming and training the mind, leading to liberation from suffering (dukkha).

- The Middle Way (The Buddha's Path): Buddha's meditation was not about extremes but about balance. The Middle Way teaches that mindfulness and meditation help one find balance, avoiding both indulgence and severe self-mortification. Meditation becomes a tool to find harmony in the mind, body, and spirit.

2. Hindu Wisdom (Yoga Sutras of Patanjali):

- Stillness of the Mind (Yoga Sutras, 1.2): Patanjali, in his *Yoga Sutras*, teaches that "Yoga is the cessation of the fluctuations of the mind." Meditation (dhyana) is the practice of quieting the mind so that it becomes steady and clear. In this state of stillness, one is able to experience the true nature of the self, which is often described as bliss, peace, or the eternal soul (Atman).

- Control over the Mind (Yoga Sutras, 1.33): Patanjali also says that one can achieve tranquility by practicing four qualities: friendliness, compassion, joy, and equanimity. These qualities help quiet the mind and reduce its tendency to wander toward negative or distracting thoughts. Through meditation, one cultivates these attitudes toward both oneself and others.

3. Taoist Wisdom (Tao Te Ching by Lao Tzu):

- Non-action and Flow (Tao Te Ching, Chapter 37): Lao Tzu, in his *Tao Te Ching*, speaks of "wu wei," which translates to "non-action" or "effortless action." Meditation in Taoism is a way to align oneself with the Tao, the natural flow of the universe. In this state of stillness, one achieves harmony by simply being, without forcing or struggling. Meditation helps the practitioner to flow with life rather than against it, finding peace in the present moment.

- The Stillness Within (Tao Te Ching, Chapter 15): Lao Tzu also writes, "The wise man is one who can remain still, and yet move with the flow of life."

Meditation allows us to access a deeper sense of stillness within ourselves, where wisdom, clarity, and insight arise naturally.

4. Ancient Greek Philosophy (Stoicism):

- Self-Mastery and Reflection (Meditations by Marcus Aurelius): While Stoicism is not strictly about meditation in the modern sense, it shares many principles. Marcus Aurelius, the Roman emperor and Stoic philosopher, wrote in his *Meditations*: "You have power over your mind, not outside events. Realize this, and you will find strength." Stoicism teaches the importance of reflection and self-control. Meditative practices in Stoicism involve reflecting on one's thoughts, actions, and the nature of the world in order to achieve tranquility and self-mastery.

5. Sufism (The Teachings of Rumi):

- The Heart's Journey (Rumi's Poetry): Rumi, a 13th-century Persian mystic and poet, taught that the heart, through meditation and prayer, can transcend the limits of the mind and experience divine love. In his poetry, he often speaks of the need to "silence the mind" to hear the whispers of the soul and the divine. For example, Rumi says, "When the soul lies down in that grass, the world is too full to talk about ideas, language, even the phrase each other—no tracings of the self remain."

Meditation, for Rumi, was about returning to the divine through the quieting of the self.

6. Indigenous Wisdom (Native American Teachings):

- The Sacredness of Silence: Many Indigenous cultures, such as the Native American traditions, recognize the power of silence and stillness as a form of spiritual practice. Meditation in these traditions is often linked to connecting with nature, the ancestors, and the spiritual world. The practice of "vision quests" or solitary reflection in nature is seen as a way of listening to the deeper wisdom of the earth and the universe. Silence and stillness are not just practices but also ways to align with sacred teachings and find clarity.

7. Christian Mysticism (The Cloud of Unknowing):

- Contemplative Prayer: In Christian mysticism, meditation is often linked with contemplative prayer—a practice of silently focusing on God's presence and surrendering the mind to divine connection. The *Cloud of Unknowing*, a medieval Christian mystical text, teaches that through meditation, one can reach a state where the "cloud" of thoughts and distractions is cleared, allowing one to experience God's love and presence. As the text suggests, "In the cloud of unknowing, lift up your heart to God."

These ancient teachings show how meditation has been seen as a universal path to personal growth, peace, and connection with something larger than oneself. By quieting the mind, we open ourselves to deeper wisdom and transformation, just as those before us have done for centuries.

## How to Start Practicing Mindfulness and Meditation

Now, let's get practical. How can you start incorporating mindfulness and meditation into your life?

### 1. Start Small

If you're new to mindfulness, start with just a few minutes of focused breathing each day. Sit in a comfortable position, close your eyes, and focus on your breath. Whenever your mind starts to wander (and it will!), gently bring your attention back to your breathing. The key here is consistency, not perfection. Even just 5 minutes of daily practice can help.

### 2. Be Present in Everyday Activities

Mindfulness doesn't just have to happen on a meditation cushion. You can practice it while walking, eating, or even washing the dishes. The goal is to bring your full attention to what you're doing without distractions. For example, if you're eating, really taste the food. Notice the texture, the flavor, and the temperature. If you're walking, pay attention to the sensation of your feet touching the ground and the sounds around you. This simple act of being fully present in each moment helps you develop a mindful mindset.

### 3. Try Guided Meditation

If sitting in silence is a bit overwhelming, try guided meditation. There are plenty of apps and videos that lead you through short meditations. These can be especially helpful for beginners because they give you a structure and guide your focus.

### 4. Practice Non-Judgmental Awareness

One of the core principles of mindfulness is non-judgment. Don't judge yourself for having distracting thoughts or feelings—just observe them. The more you practice non-judgment, the easier it becomes to accept whatever arises in your mind without reacting to it.

### 5. Set a Daily Time

Make mindfulness and meditation a part of your routine. Whether it's first thing in the morning, during lunch, or before bed, setting aside a dedicated time to practice can help you stay consistent and reap the benefits of mindfulness over time.

To help you visualize how mindfulness and meditation work, imagine your mind as a glass of muddy water. When you stir the water (i.e., when your mind is busy and chaotic), the mud swirls around, making it impossible to see clearly. But when you let the water sit still (i.e., when you meditate), the mud settles, and the water becomes clear. This is what mindfulness does—it allows the "mud" of your thoughts and emotions to settle, so you can see things with greater clarity and calm.

In today's fast-paced world, it's easy to get lost in the noise of our thoughts, emotions, and external distractions. But by practicing mindfulness and meditation, we can find stillness, clarity, and deeper self-awareness. Whether it's 5 minutes of meditation or simply being present in your daily activities, these practices are powerful tools for mental and emotional well-being. Just like Buddha's path to enlightenment, mindfulness and meditation can help you discover a greater sense of peace and freedom.

# CHAPTER 3

# Building a Self-Care Routine for Mental Well-Being: The Path to a Happier, Healthier You

Okay, let's talk about self-care. It's one of those terms that's thrown around all the time, right? You've probably seen it on Instagram with pictures of bubble baths, face masks, or maybe a cup of tea in someone's hand while they're curled up in bed. But self-care isn't just about looking cute in a bathrobe—it's a vital practice that can significantly boost your mental well-being. So, let's break it down and figure out how you can create a self-care routine that really works for you, without all the fluff.

## Why Self-Care Matters for Mental Well-Being

First things first: self-care is essential for your mental health. It's not just about pampering yourself; it's about maintaining a healthy mind, body, and soul. Think of it like putting gas in your car—it keeps everything running smoothly. When we neglect self-care, our mental health can take a hit. We get stressed, overwhelmed, and drained. But when we actively take care of ourselves, we build resilience and improve our ability to handle life's curveballs.

Let's take Liza, one of my old colleagues, as an example. She came to me feeling totally burned out. She was constantly taking care of everyone else—her family, her job, her friends—but she never carved out time for herself. She felt guilty whenever she did something for her own well-being, convinced that she was being "selfish." But after we explored the idea of self-care, she realized that by neglecting herself, she was actually doing more harm than good.

We worked together to create a routine where Liza prioritized herself, even if it was just for a few minutes a day. She started small, carving out time for walks, journaling, and even a hobby she had put on the back burner. Slowly but surely, Liza found that by taking care of herself, she was able to show up more fully for others too. Self-care is not selfish—it's necessary for your mental well-being and your ability to be there for the people you care about.

A Timeless Example of Self-Care: The Story of Jesus and Rest

When thinking about self-care, it's helpful to remember that even people with important missions and big responsibilities need time to rest and recharge. The story of Jesus in the Bible beautifully illustrates this point.

In the Gospel of Mark, Jesus and his disciples were overwhelmed with demands from people in need. Crowds followed them everywhere, and there was always work to do. Yet, in Mark 6:31, Jesus said to his disciples:

"Come with me by yourselves to a quiet place and get some rest." (Mark 6:31, NIV)

Jesus knew that taking time to rest was essential for his well-being and the effectiveness of his work. He called for a retreat, a quiet space to rejuvenate. This wasn't a luxury or a selfish act—it was a necessary part of sustaining his strength and purpose.

This story is a powerful reminder for all of us that rest and renewal are essential parts of a self-care routine. Even if we have busy lives and big responsibilities, we need to honor our need for rest, reflection, and downtime. Jesus' practice of taking a break for rest shows us that self-care allows us to keep going with renewed energy, focus, and a sense of peace.

## Building a Self-Care Routine That Works for You

So, now that we understand why self-care matters, let's figure out how to actually build a routine that fits your life. The key here is personalization. What works for one person might not work for another, and that's totally okay. Your self-care routine should be something that suits you, your lifestyle, and your needs. Ready? Let's dive in!

## 1. Start with Small, Manageable Goals

If you're someone who's never really had a self-care routine, don't go overboard and try to change everything at once. You're setting yourself up for failure if you do. Start small. Think of one or two things you can commit to each day. Maybe it's as simple as drinking more water, taking a 5-minute stretch, or stepping outside for a quick walk. These small steps can make a huge difference over time.

I remember that in the early days of my professional practice, I was struggling with anxiety and was overwhelmed. I thought that self-care meant having a full-on spa day or taking an hour-long walk every morning. But I just didn't have the time. So, I redefined self-care and started with bite-sized tasks that fit into my hectic schedule. I began doing 10-minute breathing exercises in the morning and made a habit of journaling for 5 minutes before bed. These tiny changes made a huge difference in my overall mental health. It wasn't about having an elaborate routine—it was about creating small, consistent practices that made me feel better every day.

## 2. Prioritize Mental and Physical Health

Self-care isn't just about bubble baths and Netflix binges (though both of those can be great!). It's also about taking care of your mind and body in ways that boost your overall well-being. A good self-care routine should balance both mental and physical practices.

For mental health, try things like journaling, meditation, or mindfulness. These practices can help clear your mind, reduce stress, and increase emotional clarity. Liza, for instance, started journaling as a way to process her thoughts and emotions. It gave her an outlet for everything she was carrying and helped her develop a greater sense of self-awareness.

For physical health, regular exercise, healthy eating, and getting enough sleep are key. You don't need to sign up for a marathon (unless that's your thing, of course). Even a daily walk or stretching for 10 minutes can help reduce stress, boost your mood, and improve your sleep quality.

## 3. Include Rest and Recovery Time

I get it—life's busy. But here's the thing: you need rest. Your brain and body can't function properly if you're running on empty. In fact, lack of rest is a major contributor to mental health issues like anxiety, depression, and burnout. So, make sure your self-care routine includes time for recovery and relaxation.

This doesn't have to mean hours of sleep (though that's important). It can also mean taking breaks during the day to recharge, saying no to things that drain you, or even just unplugging from your phone for a while.

## 4. Make Time for Fun and Creativity

Self-care isn't all about "getting things done" or being productive. Sometimes, the best form of self-care is simply having fun! Whether it's painting, dancing, playing a video game, or even trying a new recipe, doing something that brings you joy and sparks your creativity is a vital part of your routine.

For example, my mother found that playing the piano helped her de-stress after a long day. Even though it wasn't "productive" in the traditional sense, it brought her happiness and gave her mind a break from the daily grind. When you make time for activities that make you feel alive and energized, it's like giving your mental health a mini vacation.

## 5. Set Boundaries

One of the biggest challenges in building a self-care routine is setting boundaries. Whether it's saying no to additional tasks at work, turning off your phone during family time, or simply carving out space for yourself, boundaries are essential for mental well-being.

## The Science Behind Self-Care

Self-care isn't just a feel-good practice—it's backed by science. Studies show that regular self-care can lower cortisol levels, the hormone associated with stress, and increase serotonin, the "feel-good" chemical in the brain. For example, a 2017 study published in *Health Psychology* found that people who engaged in regular self-care reported lower stress levels and better overall health. Another study in *Psychosomatic Medicine* showed that mindfulness practices, a key part of self-care, can reduce symptoms of anxiety and depression by up to 30%. Even small acts of self-care, like taking a walk or spending time with loved ones, can boost your immune system and improve your mood. So, when you prioritize self-care, you're not just pampering yourself—you're investing in your long-term health.

## A Balanced Self-Care Routine: A Visual Guide

Self-care isn't one-size-fits-all. Think of it like a pie chart—each slice represents a different area of your life that needs attention. A balanced self-care routine includes mental, physical, emotional, and social practices. When one slice is neglected, the whole pie feels off. Use a chart as a guide to assess where you might need to focus more energy.

Mental Self-Care: Activities like journaling, meditation, or reading.

Physical Self-Care: Exercise, healthy eating and sleep.

Emotional Self-Care: Practices like therapy, setting boundaries, or expressing emotions.

Social Self-Care: Spending time with loved ones, joining a community, or volunteering.

## Overcoming Common Barriers to Self-Care

Let's be honest—self-care isn't always easy. Life gets busy, and it's easy to put yourself last. But here's the thing: self-care isn't selfish, and it doesn't have to be time-consuming. Here are some common barriers and how to overcome them:

1. Guilt: Many people feel guilty for taking time for themselves. But remember, self-care isn't a luxury

– it's a necessity. When you take care of yourself, you're better equipped to care for others. Start small, and remind yourself that you deserve this.

2.  Lack of Time: If you're short on time, focus on micro self-care practices. Even 5 minutes of deep breathing or a quick stretch can make a difference. Self-care doesn't have to be elaborate—it just has to be consistent.

3.  Feeling Overwhelmed: If the idea of starting a self-care routine feels overwhelming, break it down into tiny steps. Choose one practice to focus on this week, and build from there. Progress, not perfection, is the goal.

4.  Not Knowing Where to Start: Make a checklist to identify practices that feel manageable and meaningful to you. Experiment with different activities until you find what works best for your lifestyle and needs.

The key to a successful self-care routine is consistency. It's not about doing everything perfectly; it's about showing up for yourself every day. Don't expect instant results—mental health, like physical health, takes time to improve. Be patient and kind to yourself as you experiment with different self-care practices.

And remember, self-care isn't just a "one-and-done" deal. It's an ongoing process. Your needs might change from day to day, so be flexible and adjust your routine as needed.

The more you tune into what your body and mind need, the better you'll feel in the long run.

Building a self-care routine for mental well-being isn't just a trendy thing to do – it's an essential practice that helps you stay emotionally healthy, balanced, and resilient. By prioritizing small, manageable steps that nurture your mind and body, you can create a routine that supports your well-being in a sustainable way. Remember, self-care isn't selfish – it's an investment in yourself that pays off in so many ways. So, go ahead and take that first step toward building a routine that works for you. You deserve it!

# CHAPTER 4

# Understanding Anxiety and Depression

**Dwayne "The Rock" Johnson: Overcoming Anxiety and Depression**

When you think of Dwayne Johnson, aka "The Rock," what comes to mind? Buff, charming, and generally impossible to dislike, right? Whether he's in the ring or on the big screen, the man exudes strength—physically, emotionally, and mentally. But what if I told you that behind the muscles and megawatt smile, The Rock has also battled anxiety and depression? Yep. Even the guy who could probably benchpress your entire life is not immune to mental health struggles.

It might sound shocking, but this is a real thing. The Rock, despite his fame, fortune, and *obviously* Herculean physique, struggled with the kind of emotional battles many of us can relate to. There was even a time when the weight of it all made him consider suicide.

But here's the important takeaway: mental health challenges don't care how many Instagram followers you have or how much money you make. They can affect anyone, regardless of how strong or put-together they seem.

Johnson's "aha!" moment came when he realized that no one is meant to face this stuff alone. So, he got real with himself—and with the world. Therapy became a game-changer. The man who's used to facing opponents in the ring learned how to face his own feelings head-on. And here's the kicker: by opening up, he found strength, not weakness. His vulnerability became his superpower.

And let's not forget about self-care. For Dwayne, lifting weights and running became more than just a way to stay in shape—it was a lifeline. It turns out that lifting dumbbells can also help lift your mood. Who knew?

But perhaps most importantly, The Rock leaned into his support system. His family and friends became his emotional safety net, proving that even the toughest people need a squad to help them through the storm. Oh, and journaling? Yep, that helped too.

By sharing his story, Johnson has become a huge advocate for mental health awareness. He's using his platform to remind everyone that their mental health is just as important as their physical health—and asking for help is *not* a sign of weakness. In fact, it's a sign of strength.

**Understanding Anxiety and Depression**

Alright, let's get down to business. What exactly is anxiety and depression? And, more importantly, why does understanding them matter?

We hear these words tossed around a lot, but they're more than just a bad day or feeling stressed. Anxiety and depression are real, persistent mental health conditions that mess with how we think, feel, and function.

But here's the good news – understanding them is the first step in kicking their butts.

*What is Anxiety?*

We've all been there: sweaty palms before a presentation or worrying about a deadline that's closer than you'd like. That's anxiety, but only the tip of the iceberg. Anxiety is that nagging feeling of dread, the one that sticks around even when there's no immediate danger. It can make your heart race, your thoughts spiral, and your body feel like it's been through a workout—without actually moving.

Anxiety can look like:

- A heart that feels like it's trying to escape your chest.

- Trembling or sweating (no, not from the workout you *definitely* didn't do).

- Feeling constantly tired—even after a full night's sleep (which, spoiler alert, probably didn't happen because you were up all night thinking about everything).

- An upset stomach, which isn't as fun as it sounds.

It's not just in your head. Anxiety messes with your body, too. But it also messes with your thoughts—like constantly overthinking, jumping to the worst-case scenario, or imagining the future is about to implode.

*What is Depression?*

Depression isn't just a case of the "blues" after a bad day. It's like a fog that takes over your brain and your body, turning everything gray and flat. When you're dealing with depression, everything feels harder. The things you used to enjoy? They don't bring joy anymore. And that low energy? Even just getting out of bed can feel like a marathon.

You might notice:

- A deep sense of sadness or emptiness that sticks around longer than you'd like.

- Losing interest in stuff that once made you feel alive—whether that's your favorite hobby or your favorite person.

- Trouble sleeping, or sleeping *too* much (because it's easier to escape into dreamland than face reality).

- A lack of energy, even after getting a full night of rest (see above: a marathon, not happening).

Depression can also get inside your head, making you feel like you're worthless or just plain bad at life. It's exhausting, and it makes everything feel… heavier.

*How Anxiety and Depression Overlap*

Now, let's talk about the "two-for-one special" – when anxiety and depression team up. Spoiler alert: it's not the kind of team-up you want. Imagine trying to function with anxiety constantly running on a loop in your head while depression tells you that nothing matters. It's a recipe for feeling completely overwhelmed. You might lie awake worrying about everything under the sun, but still find it impossible to drag yourself out of bed the next day. Fun, right?

In fact, research shows that about 50% of people with depression also experience anxiety. It's like they're both at the same brain party, and neither knows when to leave.

**Everyday Stress vs. Clinical Anxiety and Depression**

So, how do you know if you're dealing with regular stress or something more serious? Here's the difference:

- **Everyday Stress/Sadness:** We all go through rough patches. You feel down after a breakup, a bad day at work, or a missed opportunity. But once the event passes, so do those feelings.

- **Clinical Anxiety/Depression:** These conditions aren't just triggered by one bad event—they linger. They show up uninvited and stick around long after the "thing" is over. If these feelings are interfering with your daily life and lasting for weeks or months, it might be time to get some help.

**Why Understanding Matters**

Understanding anxiety and depression isn't about labeling yourself or giving yourself a mental health diagnosis (because, let's be honest, no one really wants to be a "case study"). It's about recognizing what's going on so you can take steps to feel better. Therapy, self-care, lifestyle changes—they all work, but first, you've got to understand what you're dealing with.

## Strategies for Managing Anxiety and Depression

Now, let's move on to some strategies. It's not about magically flipping a switch and—bam! —no more anxiety or depression (if only it were that easy). But there are some tools and habits that can make a big difference over time. Let's dive in:

### 1. Mindfulness and Grounding Techniques

Mindfulness is like a cheat code for your brain. It helps you stay in the moment, instead of spiraling into what could go wrong or what you might've messed up in the past. Here's how you can practice mindfulness:

- **Deep Breathing:** Inhale for four seconds, hold it for four, and exhale for four. You're basically giving your nervous system a mini vacation.

- **5-4-3-2-1 Technique:** This grounding exercise is like a mental scavenger hunt. Find 5 things you can see, 4 things you can touch, 3 things you can hear, 2 things you can smell, and 1 thing you can taste. It snaps you back to reality when everything else feels like a blur.

- **Body Scan Meditation:** Lie down, get comfy, and work your way from head to toe, noticing where you're tense and consciously relaxing.

### 2. Cognitive–Behavioral Techniques

This is like your brain's personal trainer. Cognitive-behavioral therapy (CBT) helps you kick those negative thought patterns to the curb. Here's how you can start:

- **Notice Your Negative Thoughts:** Write them down if it helps. Sometimes, seeing them on paper makes you realize how dramatic they really are.

- **Challenge Those Thoughts:** Ask yourself, "Is this true?" and "Is there evidence?" Spoiler: the answer is usually no.

- **Reframe:** Turn your negative thoughts into more balanced ones. Instead of thinking, "I'm terrible at this," try, "I'm learning, and that's okay."

### 3. Lifestyle Changes

You can't just think your way out of anxiety and depression—sometimes, you've got to act your way out of it. Small daily changes can make a big difference:

- **Exercise:** Endorphins are your best friends. Even a quick walk can help lift your mood.

- **Sleep:** Prioritize your rest. Your brain is a lot more fun to live with when it's properly rested.

- **Nutrition:** Put good stuff in your body—it helps your brain stay sharp and happy.

- **Limit Stimulants:** Too much caffeine or alcohol can make anxiety worse, so try cutting back.

## *4. Seek Professional Help*

There's no shame in asking for help. Whether it's therapy, medication, or both, seeking professional support can be one of the best decisions you ever make.

## Jonny Benjamin's Journey: From Despair to Hope

Jonny Benjamin is a mental health advocate and speaker, but his journey to recovery from depression and anxiety is nothing short of remarkable. His story is especially powerful because it shows how reaching out for help and finding a sense of connection can transform one's life.

Jonny had struggled with depression and anxiety for much of his life, but it reached a crisis point in 2008 when he was 20 years old. At this time, Jonny was overwhelmed by feelings of hopelessness, isolation, and despair. He felt trapped in a dark place, unable to see any way out of his mental suffering. He had no motivation to keep going, and his thoughts became consumed by the idea of ending his life.

One fateful day, Jonny stood on London's Blackfriars Bridge with the intention of ending it all. As he stood there, paralyzed by his inner turmoil, he was approached by a stranger who noticed his distress. This stranger, a man who Jonny would later call his "guardian angel," spoke to him, offering words of comfort and kindness.

But Jonny still felt like there was no escape from his pain, and he went ahead with his plan. However, this stranger was persistent and refused to give up on him. After a few minutes of talking, Jonny changed his mind and stepped back from the edge.

This life-saving encounter planted the seeds of healing in Jonny's life. He later sought professional help for his mental health struggles. With therapy, medication, and support from his friends and family, Jonny began his journey of recovery. He still faced difficult days, but he started to find ways to manage his anxiety and depression. The key was learning that he didn't have to face his mental health challenges alone.

Jonny's life truly began to change when he decided to share his story with the world. He wanted to raise awareness about mental health and help others who were struggling in silence. He used his experience to encourage others to reach out for help and talk about their struggles openly.

In 2014, Jonny took a major step in his healing journey when he launched an emotional campaign called #FindMike. Jonny had never been able to track down the stranger who had saved his life on that bridge, so he turned to social media to find him. He shared his story and asked the public to help him find the person who had shown him kindness at his darkest moment.

Remarkably, five years later, after a lot of media attention and support from people all around the world, Jonny was able to reunite with the stranger, who was named Mike. The reunion was an emotional and powerful moment, and it helped Jonny realize just how much the kindness of a single person could impact someone's life.

## Becoming a Mental Health Advocate

Jonny now dedicates his life to speaking about mental health. He is an advocate for better mental health care, aiming to reduce stigma and encourage open conversations. Through his story, he has inspired many people to seek help and find hope in their own battles with anxiety and depression.

He has worked with various organizations to promote mental health awareness and has become a well-known face in the movement to break the silence around mental health issues.

# CHAPTER 5

# Building Resilience Through Mindset

Alright, let's talk about mindset—because how you think about challenges can make all the difference. Think of your mindset as the lens through which you see the world. If that lens is cracked or foggy, everything looks harder than it needs to be. But if you clean it up and adjust the focus, suddenly things start to look a lot more manageable.

## The Power of a Growth Mindset

You've probably heard the term "growth mindset" before, but what does it actually mean? In simple terms, it's the belief that you can grow, learn, and improve, no matter what life throws at you. It's the opposite of a fixed mindset, which says, "I'm just bad at this," or "I'll never get better," or even "This is how I am, and I am not going to change because I am good, like this."

But the research shows that people with a growth mindset are more resilient. They see setbacks as opportunities to learn, not as proof that they're doomed to fail. So, if you've ever thought, "I'm just not good at handling stress," guess what? You can get better. It's like leveling up in a video game—you just need the right strategies and a little practice.

## Reframing Setbacks

One of the best ways to build resilience is to reframe setbacks. Instead of seeing them as failures, try seeing them as feedback. For example:

Instead of: "I messed up. I'm terrible at this," you can try: "Okay, that didn't go as planned. What can I learn from this?"

This shift in perspective can make a huge difference. It's like turning a "Game Over" screen into a "Try Again" button. And the more you practice, the easier it gets.

The Story of Gandhi: Resilience Through a Positive Mindset

Mahatma Gandhi is one of the most resilient figures in history. Gandhi's life was far from easy. He faced countless challenges, from personal struggles to leading a nation in its fight for independence. But what set him apart was his unwavering positive mindset and his ability to turn adversity into opportunity.

Gandhi believed in the power of nonviolence and truth, even when the odds were stacked against him. He faced imprisonment, violence, and constant criticism, but he never lost sight of his vision. Instead of seeing these challenges as roadblocks, he saw them as stepping stones. Every setback became a chance to strengthen his resolve and refine his approach.

One of Gandhi's most famous quotes is, "Be the change that you wish to see in the world." This wasn't just a catchy slogan—it was a mindset. Gandhi understood that resilience starts from within. By focusing on what he could control—his own actions, thoughts, and attitudes—he was able to inspire millions and create lasting change.

Gandhi's story is a powerful reminder that resilience isn't about avoiding challenges; it's about facing them with a positive mindset and a clear sense of purpose. When you focus on what you can control and stay true to your values, you can overcome even the toughest obstacles.

**Self-Compassion and Positive Self-Talk**

Another key part of building resilience is being kind to yourself. Let's face it: we're often our own worst critics. But beating yourself up over every mistake doesn't help – it just makes things harder. Instead, try practicing self-compassion. Treat yourself the way you'd treat a friend who's going through a tough time.

Here are a few examples of positive self-talk:

- Instead of: "I'm such a failure."
- Try: "I'm doing the best I can, and that's enough."
- Instead of: "I'll never get this right."
- Try: "I'm learning, and that's what matters."

Self-compassion can reduce stress, improve emotional resilience and even boost physical health. So, cut yourself some slack—you're doing better than you think.

## Laughter as a Resilience Tool

Finally, don't underestimate the power of laughter. Yes, laughter. It's like a reset button for your brain. When you can find humor in a tough situation, it takes the edge off and helps you see things from a different perspective.

For example, imagine you're stuck in traffic and running late. Instead of stressing out, try laughing at the absurdity of it all. (Extra points if you crank up your favorite song and have a mini dance party in the car.) It won't change the situation, but it will change how you feel about it.

Building Resilience: Insights from SEALs and Olympic Athletes

Resilience – the ability to bounce back from setbacks, stay focused in the face of adversity, and maintain composure during high-stress situations – is a crucial trait that successful people in demanding fields cultivate. Navy SEALs and Olympic athletes are two of the most extreme examples of individuals who train and perform under intense pressure. Despite their different environments, they share a common approach to building and maintaining resilience. Let's explore the practical strategies they use.

# 1. Mental Toughness Training: Adapting the Mindset of a SEAL

Navy SEALs are the pinnacle of mental toughness. They are often called upon to perform missions under incredibly stressful, life-threatening conditions. To perform at such high levels, SEALs train their minds to stay focused, composed, and determined, even in the face of overwhelming challenges.

## a. Embracing Discomfort

One of the core aspects of SEAL training is deliberately seeking out and enduring discomfort. This could be cold water immersion, sleep deprivation, or pushing through extreme physical exhaustion during training. The idea is that by experiencing and overcoming discomfort regularly, you learn to control your emotional and physical reactions to stress.

For example, the famous "Hell Week" during SEAL training pushes candidates to their physical and emotional limits. This week is characterized by relentless physical challenges and minimal sleep. SEALs use this experience to teach themselves that they can endure nearly anything. In terms of building resilience, this practice serves as a reminder that discomfort is temporary and that persistence in the face of adversity leads to growth.

## b. The "20X Rule"

Jocko Willink, a former Navy SEAL and leadership expert, advocates for the "20X Rule," which states that when you think you're at your limit—whether physically or mentally—you're actually only at about 40% of your potential. The key to resilience is recognizing that you are capable of far more than you realize. When facing tough situations, SEALs push beyond their initial limits, knowing that they can always dig deeper.

This mindset is essential for building resilience: when you think you can't go any further, you remind yourself that you are capable of so much more, and that the breakthrough often comes right after the breaking point.

## 2. Consistency and Preparation: The Olympic Athlete's Approach

Olympic athletes, like SEALs, spend years training their minds and bodies to reach the peak of human performance. However, their resilience-building strategies are particularly focused on consistency, mental preparation, and learning from failure.

### a. Visualization

Many Olympic athletes use a technique called visualization, or mental imagery, to build resilience. This involves vividly imagining themselves succeeding in their events, but also experiencing and overcoming challenges that might arise during the competition. By mentally rehearsing their performance, athletes create a mental blueprint for success.

Michael Phelps, the most decorated Olympian of all time, famously used visualization techniques before each race. He would picture every aspect of the race in his mind, from the dive into the pool to the exact moment he touched the wall. By visualizing success, athletes prepare their minds to handle the pressure of competition and build mental resilience in the process.

## b. Embracing Setbacks

Olympic athletes know that setbacks—whether it's an injury, a disappointing performance, or a mistake during training—are inevitable. What separates resilient athletes from others is their ability to view setbacks as opportunities for growth rather than as failures.

Take Usain Bolt, for example. Before becoming the fastest man in the world, Bolt experienced numerous setbacks in his career, including injuries and disappointing performances. However, he didn't let these obstacles define him. Instead, he used them to fuel his drive, coming back stronger each time. He once said, "Don't think about the start of the race. Think about the ending."

Resilient athletes focus on their long-term goals, not on short-term failures. They acknowledge the disappointment but keep their eyes on the prize. This ability to maintain perspective in the face of setbacks is key to building resilience.

## c. Building a Routine

Olympic athletes often thrive on strict routines and habits that help them stay disciplined and resilient. Whether it's a consistent sleep schedule, a well-structured training program, or a balanced diet, creating a predictable routine minimizes uncertainty and helps athletes focus on their goals.

In fact, many athletes, like tennis star Serena Williams, rely on rituals before competitions. These rituals—whether it's listening to a specific song, doing a set warm-up routine, or repeating affirmations—help athletes feel in control and reduce pre-competition anxiety. By having these structured routines in place, athletes feel prepared to handle any stress or pressure that may arise.

## 3. The Power of Mindfulness and Focus: SEALs and Olympic Athletes

Both Navy SEALs and Olympic athletes use mindfulness and focus techniques to enhance their performance and build resilience. Resilience isn't just about enduring pain or suffering; it's also about maintaining a calm, clear mind in the most chaotic situations.

### a. The SEALs' "Box Breathing"

SEALs practice a technique called "box breathing" to control their stress response and regain composure during intense moments. Box breathing is a simple exercise that involves inhaling for a count of four, holding for four, exhaling for four, and holding again for four. This helps reset the nervous system, reduce anxiety, and refocus the mind. This practice is often used in combat situations, as well as when SEALs need to steady themselves during high-pressure moments in training or operations.

b. Olympic Athletes and Focus Under Pressure

Olympic athletes must train to stay fully present in the moment and avoid distractions, especially during high-stakes events. For instance, during a race, swimmers like Michael Phelps or runners like Allyson Felix have to block out the noise from the crowd, the pressure of expectations, and any negative thoughts. This is where mindfulness techniques come in.

In Olympic sports, mindfulness is crucial for staying in the zone. It involves focusing entirely on the task at hand, without letting anxiety about potential failure or the outcome of the competition take over. Resilient athletes learn how to quiet the mental chatter, maintain concentration, and perform at their best when it counts most.

## 4. Team Support: How SEALs and Olympic Athletes Leverage Relationships

While individual achievement is often highlighted in both the SEALs and Olympic athletes, both groups understand the value of having a solid support system.

a. SEALs' Brotherhood

One of the most powerful resilience-building tools for SEALs is the concept of brotherhood. Throughout their rigorous training, SEALs bond closely with their teammates, forming deep trust and reliance on one another. This sense of camaraderie is vital in tough situations—whether on a mission or during training. When one teammate falters, the others pick them up, and when the group faces adversity, they push through together.

In this way, SEALs rely on each other's strengths to compensate for personal weaknesses. Having a strong support system in place helps build resilience, as each person has the backing of a team that believes in them.

b. Olympic Athletes and Coaches

Similarly, Olympic athletes often rely on their coaches, trainers, and teammates for emotional and strategic support. Many athletes have mentors who guide them through the ups and downs of competition. Coaches, in particular, help athletes stay focused, fine-tune their performance, and provide perspective after setbacks.

Furthermore, the Olympic Games themselves foster a unique environment where athletes support one another, even if they are competitors. This sense of solidarity is especially apparent in team events, where success depends on the cohesion of every member, or in training camps, where athletes learn from each other's experiences.

**Practical Resilience Strategies for Anyone**

Whether it's the unyielding determination of a Navy SEAL or the unwavering focus of an Olympic athlete, the strategies they employ to build resilience can be applied to anyone facing challenges. These strategies include embracing discomfort, pushing through perceived limits, practicing mindfulness, learning from setbacks, creating routines, and relying on a supportive team.

While Navy SEALs and Olympic athletes operate in extreme environments, their resilience-building practices have universal applications. Resilience isn't just about "toughing it out" – it's about mental training, emotional awareness, and building the habits that help you thrive under pressure. By adopting some of these practical strategies, anyone can become more resilient and better equipped to handle life's inevitable challenges.

# CHAPTER 6

## Be Kind to Yourself

Okay, let's get real for a second. How often do you catch yourself talking to yourself like you're the worst person in the world? Maybe you look in the mirror and think, "Ugh, why did I eat that entire pizza last night?" or "Why can't I just be more productive, like everyone else?" (Seriously, when did we all get so obsessed with being productive 24/7?)

Guess what? It's time to stop. I mean, we've all heard the "treat others how you want to be treated" mantra, right? Well, when was the last time you treated yourself with a little kindness? You totally deserve it. And here's the kicker – it's actually good for your mental health. Who knew?

In this chapter, we're going to talk about how being kind to yourself is not only a game-changer for your well-being, but can also make you feel like a whole new person. So grab your favorite beverage, put on your comfiest socks, and let's dive into the art of self-compassion.

What's the Deal with Self-Compassion?

Self-compassion is like your inner cheerleader who doesn't just root for you when you win, but also gives you a big hug when you trip over your own two feet (we've all been there, right?).

**Self-compassion is made up of three simple ingredients:**

1. Self-Kindness: Instead of yelling at yourself like a drill sergeant when you make a mistake (we've all done it, no judgment), you treat yourself like a good friend who's having a rough day. You don't yell at your friend, do you? You hug them and say, "It's okay, you've got this!"

2. Common Humanity: You're not alone in this messy human experience. Everyone makes mistakes, has bad days, and feels like they're not doing enough at times. It's literally part of being human. So stop thinking you're the only one struggling! Join the club.

3. Mindfulness: This is the tricky part – being aware of your thoughts without spiraling into a black hole of self-criticism. Mindfulness is like observing your inner monologue from a distance, nodding and saying, "Oh, okay, I see you there, negative thoughts. But I'm not going to let you ruin my day."

When you combine these three things, you've got a pretty awesome recipe for self-compassion. And it's like the secret cheat code to make life just a little bit easier.

## Why Does Being Nice to Ourselves Matter?

So, why is being nice to yourself such a big deal? Why should we stop beating ourselves up every time we make a mistake or forget to buy more toilet paper? Let's break it down:

1. Less Stress: You know that feeling when your boss sends you an email that starts with, "Let's talk about this," and your stomach drops into your shoes? (Just me? Okay.) When we're kind to ourselves, we actually lower the amount of cortisol (the stress hormone) in our bodies. Instead of panicking about every little thing, we're like, "Okay, it's not the end of the world. Let's deal with this like a grown-up."

2. More Resilience: Think of self-compassion as building muscle. The more you use it, the stronger you get. When you're kind to yourself during tough times, you build resilience. Instead of saying, "I suck," you think, "Alright, this is hard, but I'm going to learn from this and keep going." Suddenly, life's obstacles don't seem quite as scary.

3. Better Self-Esteem: You know that old saying, "You can't pour from an empty cup"? Well, if you're constantly draining your mental and emotional cup by being harsh on yourself, you're going to run on empty. But when you practice self-compassion, you fill your cup back up. And guess what? You start to like the person looking back at you in the mirror a little bit more. And who doesn't want that?

4.  Better Mental Health: Studies show that people who practice self-compassion experience less anxiety, depression, and loneliness. When you stop berating yourself for every little thing, your mental health starts to improve. It's like giving your brain a little vacation. And who doesn't want a brain that feels relaxed and happy?

## Buddhist Monks: The Self-Kindness Experts

Now, let's talk about some people who really know how to practice self-compassion. I'm talking about Buddhist monks. These folks have been practicing the art of kindness to themselves for centuries, and they've got it down to an art form.

Buddhist monks practice something called metta—loving-kindness. And get this: they don't just use it for others; they start by being loving and kind to themselves. It's like starting with the basics before you go out and spread the good vibes to everyone else.

One of their main practices is called "loving-kindness meditation," where they sit quietly and repeat phrases like, "May I be happy, may I be safe, may I be healthy, may I live with ease." It's like giving yourself a mental hug, and guess what? It works. Monks who practice this meditation report feeling more peaceful, more connected to others, and happier.

But wait, there's more! The Dalai Lama, one of the most famous Buddhist figures, often talks about the importance of self-compassion. He's basically the OG of kindness, and he says that you can't truly offer love and compassion to others until you've mastered it with yourself. So, take notes – if it works for the Dalai Lama, it might just work for you.

## How to Be Kind to Yourself (Without Feeling Weird About It)?

Now that we know why self-compassion is basically a superpower, let's see how you can practice it without feeling like you're in a cheesy self-help commercial. Here are some super easy, no-fuss ways to show yourself some love:

1. Talk to Yourself Like You're Your Best Friend: The next time you mess up, don't go full drama queen on yourself. Instead, say something like, "Okay, that didn't go as planned. But hey, nobody's perfect. Let's try again tomorrow." It's like having your own personal cheerleader, but with way fewer pom-poms.

2. Mindful Breathing: When life's giving you lemons (or when your boss asks you for that report again), just breathe. Seriously. Take a deep breath in, hold it for a second, and then slowly let it out. This simple act can ground you and help you stop spiraling.

3. Take Breaks Without Guilt: I know it feels like you're supposed to be working non-stop, but your brain isn't a robot. It needs breaks. So take them! Whether it's a 10-minute walk outside or a five-minute dance party in your living room (don't lie, we all do it), give yourself permission to recharge.

4. Give Yourself a Pass: Sometimes, you're going to mess up. It's part of being human. Instead of throwing yourself a pity party, say, "Okay, that was a hiccup. I'll learn from it and move on." And then actually move on. No guilt, no shame. Just forward momentum.

5. Gratitude Journal: You don't have to write an essay about your gratitude, but jotting down a few things you're thankful for can help shift your mindset. And trust me, there's always something to be grateful for—even if it's just your favorite snack.

**Wrapping It Up: Be Your Own BFF**

Being kind to yourself isn't just a nice idea—it's an essential part of taking care of your mental health. When you practice self-compassion, you reduce stress, build resilience, and improve your self-esteem. And who doesn't want to feel like their best self, right?

So, next time you catch yourself in a spiral of self-criticism, remember the Buddhist monks (and the Dalai Lama, if we're being honest). They've been practicing self-compassion for centuries, and look how peaceful and happy they are. If they can do it, so can you. Be kind to yourself, treat yourself with the same love you show others, and watch your mental health improve.

And remember, you're not alone. We're all human. We all mess up. But that doesn't mean we aren't worthy of kindness, compassion, and, yes, even a little bit of fun along the way.

You've got this. And guess what? You're amazing.

# CHAPTER 7

# You are What You Feed Your Mind (And Your Body, Too)

We all know this but don't always like to admit: what you feed into your body and mind totally affects your mood, mental health, and pretty much every aspect of your life. I mean, we've all heard the phrase "You are what you eat," but let's throw in a twist—you are what you watch, listen to, and think about. Intrigued? Well, buckle up, because this chapter is about to get delicious—both for your body and soul.

Mental Junk Food: The News, Gossip, and All That Negative Stuff

Let's start with a classic culprit: the news. Ah, yes, the never-ending rollercoaster of drama, chaos, and crisis that greets you every morning when you open your phone. Does it make you feel totally zen? Probably not. More like you're one headline away from a mini existential crisis, right?

If you're feeding your brain a steady diet of negative headlines, tragic stories, and 24/7 conflict, don't be surprised if your mental health starts feeling like it's been hit by a truck. I mean, your brain is like a sponge, soaking up whatever it's exposed to. So, if your daily news routine includes more doom than a doomsday prepper, your thoughts are probably starting to get a little, well, doom-y too.

Buddha actually had some wisdom here. He said, "What you think, you become." In other words, if you're constantly consuming negativity, your brain will marinate in it until it starts showing up in your thoughts and actions. So, stop for a second—how does your media diet make you feel? If you're swimming in a sea of bad news, maybe it's time to add some positive news into the mix.

I know, I know—positive news can sometimes feel like spotting a unicorn in a field of actual real horses, but it exists! There are plenty of heartwarming, inspiring stories out there. Subscribe to a feel-good newsletter, watch uplifting TED talks, or just follow accounts that bring joy to your feed. Trust me, your brain will thank you.

Good Conversations = Happy Brain

Now, let's talk about something equally important—your conversations. Ever had that one friend who can turn any conversation into a complaint-fest or a pity party? Yeah, they're fun… until they're not. But here's the thing: the kind of conversations you engage in directly impact how you feel. If you're constantly surrounded by negativity, criticism, and drama, it's like you're feeding your brain a full-course meal of mental junk food.

But guess what? The opposite is also true. Good conversations—conversations filled with laughter, positivity, and love—are like feeding your brain a mental smoothie packed with kale and sunshine. Well, maybe without the kale, if you're not into that, but you get the idea. When you talk about things that uplift you or discuss exciting, motivating ideas with friends or colleagues, your brain gets a boost of dopamine, and guess what that means? Less stress and more happiness. And who doesn't want that?

Start surrounding yourself with people who uplift and inspire you. Talk about what's going right in your life. Don't be afraid to laugh about the silly stuff (even if it's just your latest attempt at baking sourdough bread that somehow turned out like a brick). You'll start feeling like your mental diet is filled with dessert instead of veggies (unless you like veggies—no judgment here).

Positive Thoughts = Positive You

Your thoughts are literally what create your reality. You know how when you're stuck in a bad mood, everything seems to go wrong? You stub your toe on the coffee table, spill your drink, and then the car doesn't start? That's what happens when your brain is flooded with negative thoughts – it's like a self-fulfilling prophecy.

But here's the cool part: you can train your brain to think in more positive, productive ways. It's kind of like switching from a fast-food mindset (hello, instant gratification!)

to a gourmet, balanced meal (hello, mental clarity and peace!). Buddha, the original mindfulness guru, said it best: "What you think, you become." So, if you want to feel good, start thinking good.

Of course, this isn't about ignoring real problems or pretending everything is perfect. But the way you react to challenges can make all the difference. Instead of spiraling into negative thoughts, try flipping the script. Ask yourself, "What's the lesson here? What can I learn from this?"

Even if you don't have a perfect answer, simply reframing your thoughts will keep your brain from getting stuck in the mud. And trust me, the more you practice this, the better it gets. You'll start noticing that things don't seem as overwhelming. Plus, you'll have a lot less mental junk food to deal with.

## The Body: Feeding It with Goodness, Too

Alright, enough about the brain for a second. Let's dive into the other important thing that impacts your mental health: your body. You might be thinking, "Okay, so what does the salad I eat have to do with my mood?" Oh, everything, my friend.

Let's break it down. Your body and mind are connected—no, seriously, they're like a two-for-one deal. If you treat your body like a trash can (i.e., bingeing on chips and soda all day), your brain's going to feel it. And not in a good way. You'll start feeling sluggish, irritable, and probably a little down. Your brain will be all like, "What's going on? Why do I feel so meh?"

But when you feed your body with nutritious foods—fruits, veggies, lean proteins, and good fats—your brain gets the nutrients it needs to function at its best. It's like upgrading from a flip phone to the latest smartphone. Suddenly, your brain's firing on all cylinders, and you feel more energized, focused, and ready to take on the world. Plus, those good vibes will spill over into your mental health.

And don't forget the importance of movement. You don't have to run a marathon or become a yoga guru overnight (unless you want to, of course). But moving your body—even a 10-minute walk—releases endorphins, the magical happiness hormones. So, get your body moving, even if it's just dancing in your living room like nobody's watching. Trust me, your brain will thank you.

**The Buddha Way: Mindfulness and Self-Care**

You know how we've been talking about feeding your mind and body well? Buddha was way ahead of us on this one. He taught that mindfulness is key to a happy life. In simple terms, mindfulness is paying attention to what you're feeding your mind in the present moment.

Buddha said, "Health is the greatest gift, contentment the greatest wealth, faithfulness the best relationship." It's like he was handing out self-care tips centuries before it became a thing on Instagram. When you feed your mind with positive thoughts, when you're kind to your body, and when you practice mindfulness, you start to feel more at peace with yourself and the world around you. And that, my friend, is the ultimate mental health win.

Feed your brain, feed your body, and feed your soul with good stuff. Watch what you consume—whether it's news, conversations, food, or thoughts. If you want a happier, healthier mind, start with the basics: positive news, positive conversations, and positive thoughts. Oh, and don't forget to throw in some veggies, a little exercise, and a good laugh here and there.

Because guess what? You're in control of what you feed yourself. So, why not choose the mental equivalent of a delicious, nourishing buffet rather than the junk food line? Your body, mind, and spirit will thank you.

And Buddha would probably give you a high five (if he could).

# CHAPTER 8

# The Power of Gratitude –
# Transforming Your Mindset

By gratitude, I don't mean the kind of gratitude where you half-heartedly mutter "thank you" when someone holds the door for you (though that's nice too). I'm talking about *real* gratitude—the kind that makes you stop in your tracks, smile at the sky, and think, "Wow, life is pretty amazing."

Gratitude isn't just a fluffy concept for self-help books. It's a game-changer for your mental health. When you practice gratitude, you're not ignoring life's challenges—you're choosing to focus on what's going right. And that small shift can make a world of difference.

So, let's go further deep into why gratitude matters, how it impacts your brain, and how you can start practicing it today. It's easier than you think, and the benefits are huge. Plus, I'll throw in a little wisdom from the Bible and a story from Oprah Winfrey to keep things spiritually grounded and inspiring. Let's go!

Why Gratitude Matters (Besides Making You Less Grumpy) -

Let's be real: life can be a rollercoaster. One minute, you're cruising along, and the next, you're stuck in traffic, late for work, and spilling coffee on your favorite shirt. (Why does it always land on the *white* shirt?!) But even on the worst days, there's usually something to be grateful for – a kind word from a stranger, a hilarious meme, or the fact that coffee stains are a thing of the past thanks to a stain remover.

Gratitude isn't about pretending everything's perfect. It's about finding the good, no matter how small, and letting it lift you up. And here's the thing: the more you practice gratitude, the more you'll notice those little moments of goodness. It's like training your brain to spot the silver linings. (And trust me, there are more silver linings than you think. They're just hiding behind your grumpy morning face.)

The Science of Gratitude (AKA Why Your Brain Loves It)

Okay, let's get a little science-y for a moment (but I'll keep it fun, promise). Research shows that gratitude has a huge impact on mental health.

- Boosts Happiness: Gratitude increases levels of serotonin and dopamine, the "feel-good" chemicals in your brain. It's like a natural antidepressant, but without the side effects of wanting to eat an entire pizza by yourself.

- Reduces Stress: Practicing gratitude lowers cortisol levels, the hormone associated with stress. When you're grateful, your body literally relaxes. (Take that, traffic jam!)

- Improves Relationships: Gratitude makes you more empathetic and compassionate, which strengthens your connections with others. (Pro tip: Say "thank you" to your partner more often. It works wonders, as I know from experience).

- Enhances Resilience: Grateful people bounce back from setbacks faster. They're less likely to get stuck in negative thought loops and more likely to find meaning in difficult experiences.

In short, gratitude isn't just good for your soul – it's good for your brain. And who doesn't want a happier, healthier brain?

How to Practice Gratitude (Without It Feeling Like Homework)

Now that we've established why gratitude is so important, let's talk about how to actually do it. Here are some practical (and fun) strategies to get you started:

**1. Keep a Gratitude Journal (But Make It Fun)**

One of the simplest ways to practice gratitude is to keep a gratitude journal. But let's be honest: writing "I'm grateful for my family" every day gets old fast. So, let's spice it up.

- Be Specific: Instead of writing, "I'm grateful for my family," try, "I'm grateful for the way my dog wagged his tail so hard he knocked over a lamp today." (True story. RIP lamp.)

- Add Humor: Gratitude doesn't have to be serious. Write down the silly things too, like, "I'm grateful for the person who invented pudding. You're doing the Lord's work."

- Make It Visual: Doodle, use stickers or add photos to your journal. Turn it into a creative project that makes you smile.

Pro Tip: If you're feeling stuck, think about the people, experiences, or things that make your life better. Even on tough days, there's usually something to be grateful for. (Like the fact that cool jeans exist. Seriously, where would we be without them?)

## 2. Practice Gratitude in the Moment (AKA Stop and Smell the Coffee)

Gratitude doesn't have to wait until the end of the day. You can practice it in the moment, whenever something good happens.

- Pause and Notice: When something positive happens, take a moment to really notice it. For example, if you see a beautiful sunset, stop and take it in. (Bonus points if you take a photo and caption it, "Nailed it, nature.").

- Say Thank You: Express gratitude to the people who make your life better. It could be as simple as saying, "Thank you for listening," or "I really appreciate your help." (Extra credit if you throw in a hug.)

- Savor the Good: When something good happens, savor it. Let yourself really enjoy the moment, whether it's a delicious meal or a heartfelt conversation. (And if it's a delicious meal, take a photo for your gratitude journal. #FoodieGratitude)

## 3. Reframe Challenges with Gratitude (Yes, Even Traffic Jams)

Gratitude isn't just about the good times – it's also a powerful tool for navigating challenges.

- Find the Lesson: When you're facing a tough situation, ask yourself, "What can I learn from this?" or "How is this helping me grow?" (For example, being stuck in traffic teaches you the art of car karaoke. You're welcome.)

- Focus on What's Left: Even in loss, there's often something to be grateful for. For example, if you lose a job, you might be grateful for the skills you gained or the support of your loved ones. (And the fact that you no longer have to wear pants to work. Silver lining!)

- Practice Gratitude for the Small Wins: Celebrate small victories, like getting out of bed on a tough day or making it through a difficult conversation.

## 4. Create a Gratitude Ritual (Because Rituals Are Cool)

Incorporating gratitude into your daily routine can make it a natural part of your life.

- Morning Gratitude: Start your day by thinking of three things you're grateful for. It sets a positive tone for the day ahead. (And if one of those things is coffee, you're already winning.)

- Gratitude Jar: Write down things you're grateful for on slips of paper and drop them in a jar. On tough days, pull out a few to remind yourself of the good in your life. (Bonus: Decorate the jar with glitter. Because why not?)

- Bedtime Reflection: Before you go to sleep, reflect on the good things that happened during the day. It's a great way to end the day on a positive note. (And if you fall asleep mid-reflection, that's okay too. You're still winning.)

## A Story of Gratitude: Oprah Winfrey's Gratitude Journal

If there's one person who knows the power of gratitude, it's Oprah Winfrey. Yes, *the* Oprah—media mogul, philanthropist, and queen of the inspirational quote. Oprah has been practicing gratitude for years, and she credits it as one of the key habits that transformed her life.

Oprah started keeping a gratitude journal over 20 years ago, and she's been a passionate advocate for the practice ever since. Every night, she writes down five things she's grateful for from that day. And no, it's not always big, life-changing stuff. Sometimes, it's as simple as a good meal, a beautiful sunset, or a kind word from a friend.

In her own words:

"The more you praise and celebrate your life, the more there is in life to celebrate."

Oprah's gratitude practice has helped her stay grounded, even during the busiest and most challenging times of her career. It's a reminder that gratitude isn't just for the good days – it's for *every* day. And if it works for Oprah, it can work for you too.

A Note from the Bible: Gratitude as a Way of Life

The Bible has a lot to say about gratitude, and one of my favorite verses is **1 Thessalonians 5:18**:

"Give thanks in all circumstances; for this is God's will for you in Christ Jesus."

This verse reminds us that gratitude isn't just for the good times – it's for *all* times. Even when life feels overwhelming, there's always something to be thankful for. Gratitude shifts our focus from what's wrong to what's right, and it helps us see God's hand in every situation.

So, whether you're celebrating a big win or navigating a tough day, take a moment to give thanks. It's not just good for your soul—it's a powerful way to connect with God and find peace in the midst of chaos.

## The Ripple Effect of Gratitude

Here's the beautiful thing about gratitude: it doesn't just benefit you—it benefits everyone around you. When you're grateful, you're more patient, compassionate, and present with others. It's like filling your own cup, so you have more to give.

Gratitude isn't about ignoring life's challenges or pretending everything's perfect. It's about choosing to focus on the good, even when things are tough. And that small shift can make a world of difference.

So, the next time you're feeling down, take a deep breath and think of one thing you're grateful for. It could be something big, like your health, or something small, like the smell of fresh coffee. Whatever it is, let it lift you up.

You deserve to see the good in your life. And the more you practice gratitude, the more good you'll find. (And if that good thing is chocolate cake, I fully support you.)

# CHAPTER 9

# Building Healthy Relationships – The Heart of Connection

I am going to explain about relationships - not the kind where you're stuck in a group chat with people you haven't seen since high school. It's not the boyfriend-girlfriend relationship stuff. I'm talking about *real* relationships - the kind that make you feel seen, heard, and valued. The kind that lift you up when you're down and make life's ups and downs a little easier to navigate.

Healthy relationships are the backbone of a happy, fulfilling life. They're where we find love, support, and connection. But let's be honest: relationships can also be messy, complicated, and downright frustrating at times. (Cue the dramatic sigh.)

What makes a relationship healthy? How can you build stronger connections with the people in your life? And what do you do when things get tough? It's not about being perfect – it's about being present, kind, and willing to grow.

What Makes a Relationship Healthy?

**What does a healthy relationship look like? Here are some key ingredients:**

1.  Mutual Respect: You value each other's opinions, boundaries, and individuality. (No, you don't have to agree on everything. Yes, you do have to respect each other's right to disagree.)

2.  Trust: You feel safe being yourself, knowing that the other person has your back. (And no, trust isn't built overnight. It's earned through consistent actions over time.)

3.  Communication: You talk openly and honestly, even when it's uncomfortable. (Hint: This doesn't mean yelling. It means listening and sharing in a way that fosters understanding.)

4.  Support: You're there for each other through the good times and the bad. (And yes, that includes showing up with ice cream and tissues when needed.)

5.  Independence: You maintain your own identity and interests, even as you grow together. (Because no one wants to be in a relationship with a clone of themselves.)

How to Build Healthy Relationships (Without Losing Your Mind)

Now that we know what healthy relationships look like, let's see how to build them.

## 1. Communicate Like a Pro (Not Like a Reality TV Star)

Communication is the foundation of any healthy relationship. But let's be real: it's not always easy. Here's how to do it right:

- Listen Actively: When someone is talking, really listen. Don't just wait for your turn to speak. (And no, scrolling through your phone doesn't count as listening.)

- Use "I" Statements: Instead of saying, "You never listen to me," try, "I feel unheard when I'm interrupted." It's less accusatory and more likely to lead to a productive conversation.

- Be Honest (But Kind): Honesty is important, but so is tact. You can be truthful without being hurtful. (For example, "I'm not a fan of that shirt" is better than "That shirt looks like it was designed by a blindfolded toddler.")

## 2. Set Boundaries (Because You're Not a Doormat)

Boundaries are essential for healthy relationships. They're not about building walls; they're about creating healthy space.

- Know Your Limits: What are you comfortable with? What's a hard no? Be clear about your boundaries, both with yourself and others.

- Communicate Them Clearly: Don't assume people know your boundaries. Say them out loud. (For example, "I need some alone time after work to recharge.")

- Respect Others' Boundaries: Just as you want your boundaries respected, respect others'. (No, "But I'm your best friend!" is not an excuse to ignore someone's boundaries.)

## 3. Show Appreciation (Because Everyone Loves a Compliment)

Gratitude isn't just for your journal – it's for your relationships too. Showing appreciation can strengthen your connections and make the other person feel valued.

- Say Thank You: A simple "thank you" can go a long way. (For example, "Thank you for always making me laugh.")

- Celebrate the Little Things: Notice and acknowledge the small acts of kindness. (For example, "I really appreciate how you always remember my favorite coffee order.")

- Be Specific: Instead of a generic "You're great," try, "I love how you always know how to cheer me up when I'm feeling down."

## 4. Be Present (Put Down the Phone)

In a world full of distractions, being present is one of the greatest gifts you can give someone.

- Give Your Full Attention: When you're with someone, be with them. Put down your phone, make eye contact, and really engage. (Yes, even if your Instagram feed is calling your name.)

- Show Up: Be there for the important moments, whether it's a birthday, a tough day, or just a random Tuesday. (And no, sending a text doesn't count as showing up.)

- Be Mindful: Pay attention to the little things, like their tone of voice or body language. Sometimes, what's not said is just as important as what is.

## 5. Work Through Conflict (Without Starting World War III)

Conflict is a normal part of any relationship. It's not about avoiding it – it's about handling it in a healthy way.

- Stay Calm: Take a deep breath before responding. (And no, slamming doors is not a healthy coping mechanism.)

- Focus on the Issue: Don't bring up past grievances or make personal attacks. Stick to the topic at hand.

- Find Common Ground: Look for solutions that work for both of you. (Hint: Compromise is your friend.)

A Story of Connection: Barack Obama and Joe Biden's Friendship

When it comes to healthy relationships, few examples are as inspiring as the friendship between Barack Obama and Joe Biden. What started as a professional partnership during their time in the White House has grown into a deep, enduring friendship built on mutual respect, trust, and unwavering support.

How Their Friendship Works:

- Mutual Respect: From the beginning, Obama and Biden respected each other's strengths and perspectives. Obama valued Biden's decades of political experience, while Biden admired Obama's vision and leadership. Their ability to learn from and lean on each other strengthened their bond.

- Unwavering Support: Through personal and professional challenges, they've always had each other's backs. When Biden's son Beau passed away in 2015, Obama was there to offer comfort and support. Similarly, Biden has been a steadfast advocate for Obama's legacy and vision.

- Shared Humor: One of the hallmarks of their friendship is their ability to laugh together. Their playful banter and inside jokes have become legendary, showing that even in the most serious of roles, joy and connection matter.

- Loyalty and Trust: Their friendship is rooted in trust. As Obama once said, *"Joe, you're not just a great vice president—you're a great friend."* This trust has allowed them to navigate challenges and celebrate successes together.

Obama and Biden's friendship is a reminder that healthy relationships are built on mutual respect, trust, and a willingness to support each other through thick and thin. They show us that even in high-pressure environments, it's possible to cultivate meaningful connections that stand the test of time.

## Relationships Are a Journey

Building healthy relationships isn't about being perfect – it's about being present, kind, and willing to grow. It's about showing up, even when it's hard, and choosing to connect, even when it's messy.

So, take a moment to reflect on the relationships in your life. What's working? What could use a little TLC? And what steps can you take to strengthen those connections?

Remember, relationships are a journey, not a destination. And the more love, kindness and effort you put into them, the more they'll give back to you.

# CHAPTER 10

# Finding Purpose and Passion –
# The Path to a Meaningful Life

Is there a purpose and passion in life, or do we have to find one? I am not talking about the kind of purpose that sounds like a corporate mission statement (vision and mission, etc. - yawn). I'm talking about *real* purpose—the kind that makes you jump out of bed in the morning (or at least hit snooze one less time). The kind that gives your life meaning and direction, even on the toughest days.

And passion? That's the spark that lights you up. It's what makes you lose track of time because you're so engrossed in what you're doing. It's the thing that makes you feel alive.

But here's the thing: finding your purpose and passion isn't always easy. It's not like you wake up one day with a neon sign pointing you in the right direction. (If only, right?) It's a journey—one that requires curiosity, courage, and a willingness to explore.

So, let's break it down. What is purpose? What is passion? And how can you find yours? It's not about being perfect – it's about being curious, open, and willing to take risks.

What is Purpose? (And Why Does It Matter?)

Purpose is your "why." It's the reason you get out of bed in the morning. It's what gives your life meaning and direction. And no, it doesn't have to be some grand, world-changing mission. Your purpose can be as simple as being a great parent, creating art that inspires others, or helping people in your community.

Here's why purpose matters:

- It Gives You Direction: When you know your purpose, it's easier to make decisions and set goals. (No more aimlessly scrolling through Instagram for hours.)

- It Boosts Resilience: Having a sense of purpose helps you bounce back from setbacks. (Because when you know your "why," the "how" becomes a little easier.)

- It Enhances Well-Being: Studies show that people with a strong sense of purpose are happier, healthier, and more fulfilled. (This is something we want, right?)

What is Passion? (And How Do You Find It?)

Passion is what lights you up. It's the thing you could talk about for hours, the activity that makes you lose track of time, the cause that makes your heart race. Passion is the fuel that drives you to pursue your purpose.

But here's the thing: passion isn't always obvious. Sometimes it's buried under layers of "shoulds" and "have-tos" (Like, "I should get a stable job" or "I have to be practical"). So, how do you find it?

How to Find Your Purpose and Passion (Without Losing Your Mind)

Finding your purpose and passion is a journey, not a destination. They're dynamic, shaped by our experiences, growth, and changing circumstances over time. What feels like your purpose or passion today may shift as you gain new experiences, encounter different people, or face different challenges. For example, your career might start in one direction, but over time, you might discover that your passion lies in a different field or way of helping others. This constant evolution is part of the beauty of the journey. Each step, even the setbacks or detours, adds meaning to the process. Passion and purpose aren't necessarily a final "achievement" but a continuous source of fulfillment. Once you think you've found your passion, you might realize there's more to uncover or experience, and that discovery can continue throughout life.

Here are some practical strategies to help you get started:

## 1. Reflect on What Matters to You

Take some time to think about what's important to you. What do you care about? What makes you feel alive? Here are some questions to get you started:

- What would you do if money weren't an issue?

- What problems in the world do you feel most passionate about solving?

- What activities make you lose track of time?

- What do people often compliment you on? (Hint: This could be a clue to your strengths and passions.)

## 2. Explore Your Interests

Passion often starts with curiosity. So, give yourself permission to explore. Try new things, take classes, read books, or volunteer. You never know what might spark your interest.

- Take Small Steps: You don't have to quit your job and move to Bali to find your passion. Start small. Take a cooking class, join a book club, or try a new hobby.

- Be Open to Failure: Not everything you try will be a hit – and that's okay. Failure is just part of the process. (Think of it as data collection. You're figuring out what doesn't work so you can find what does.)

## 3. Pay Attention to What Energizes You

Your body and emotions are great indicators of what lights you up. Pay attention to how you feel when you're doing different activities.

- Energy Boosters: What activities leave you feeling energized and inspired? (For example, do you feel alive after a creative project or a deep conversation?)

- Energy Drainers: What activities leave you feeling drained and depleted? (For example, do you dread certain tasks or interactions?)

## 4. Align with Your Values

Your purpose and passion are often closely tied to your values. So, take some time to identify what matters most to you. Here are some common values to consider:

- Family
- Creativity
- Service
- Growth
- Freedom
- Connection

Once you know your values, look for ways to align your life with them. For example, if connection is important to you, you might find purpose in building strong relationships or working in a people-focused career.

## 5. Take Action (Even If You're Not Sure)

Finding your purpose and passion isn't about waiting for a lightning bolt of inspiration. It's about taking action and seeing what resonates.

- Start Small: You don't have to have it all figured out. Just take one small step in the direction of your interests and values.

- Experiment: *Treat your life like a science experiment. Try different things, observe the results, and adjust as needed.

- Be Patient: Finding your purpose and passion is a journey, not a race. Give yourself permission to explore and grow.

A Story of Purpose and Passion: Arjuna and Krishna**

There is an interesting story of Arjuna, a warrior prince, and his divine guide, Lord Krishna, from the **Bhagavad Gita**. This ancient text is part of the Indian epic, the *Mahabharata*, and it offers timeless wisdom on purpose, duty, and passion.

Arjuna is a skilled archer and one of the five Pandava brothers. He finds himself on the battlefield of Kurukshetra, facing an army that includes his own relatives, teachers, and friends. The moral dilemma is overwhelming: how can he fight against people he loves and respects?

As Arjuna stands on the battlefield, he is filled with doubt and despair. He puts down his bow and turns to his charioteer, Lord Krishna, for guidance. In this moment of crisis, Krishna becomes not just a charioteer but a spiritual teacher.

Krishna explains to Arjuna that his purpose, or *dharma*, is to fight for justice and uphold righteousness. He reminds Arjuna that as a warrior, it is his duty to protect the innocent and stand against evil, even if it means facing difficult choices.

Krishna says: "You have a right to perform your prescribed duties, but you are not entitled to the fruits of your actions. Never consider yourself the cause of the results of your activities, and never be attached to not doing your duty."* (Bhagavad Gita 2:47)

Krishna's teachings help Arjuna reconnect with his passion for justice and his commitment to his role as a warrior. He realizes that his purpose is not just about personal gain or avoiding discomfort – it's about fulfilling his duty with integrity and devotion.

Arjuna's passion for righteousness reignites, and he picks up his bow, ready to fight for what is right. His journey is a powerful reminder that purpose and passion often require us to face our fears and make difficult choices.

Arjuna's story is a profound lesson in finding purpose and following passion, even when the path is unclear or challenging. Here's what we can take away from his journey:

- Purpose is Tied to Duty: Your purpose isn't always about what you *want* to do—it's about what you *need* to do. It's about fulfilling your responsibilities with integrity and dedication.

- Passion Requires Courage: Following your passion often means stepping out of your comfort zone and facing difficult situations. But when you align with your purpose, you'll find the courage to move forward.

  — Detach from Outcomes: Focus on doing your best without being attached to the results. This mindset frees you from fear and allows you to act with clarity and confidence.

## Your Purpose and Passion Are Within You

Finding your purpose and passion isn't about being perfect – it's about being curious, open, and willing to take risks. It's about exploring what lights you up and aligning your life with what matters most to you.

So, take a deep breath and start exploring. Try new things, reflect on what energizes you, and take small steps toward your dreams. Remember, your purpose and passion are within you—you just have to uncover them.

And when you do, you'll find that life feels more meaningful, fulfilling, and alive. So, what are you waiting for? Your purpose is calling.

# CHAPTER 11

# A Simple Story: The Mirage of More

The numbers glowed on the screen in front of him, a bright, nearly hypnotic display of success. Another quarter, another record profit. His empire was stronger than ever. A brief wave of satisfaction washed over him as he leaned back in his chair, the soft leather creaking beneath him. He could hear the muffled clink of glasses in the distance—his celebration had already begun downstairs, the usual champagne and congratulatory cheers from his staff.

Ryan was a man who thrived on achievement. Born into wealth, he had never known hunger or struggle, but he had built his own legacy. With a sharp mind and a relentless drive, he expanded the family business beyond what anyone thought possible. Every year, he set higher goals—targets that seemed almost unreachable—and then, without fail, shattered them. The thrill of surpassing each target had once been enough. Once.

Now, as the excitement of the latest achievement began to fade, he felt that familiar tug of something missing. He could hear the voices downstairs, but they felt distant, like background noise to the storm brewing inside him. It was the same feeling that always came after success—elation that faded too quickly, leaving only an aching emptiness in its place.

"Ryan, come and join us!" his assistant called from the door, her voice laced with excitement.

He didn't answer immediately. He stared at the numbers on his screen, a reflection of his work, his success—his everything. Yet, somehow, it felt hollow. It was always the same. Every victory felt like a fleeting moment of euphoria, and soon, it was replaced by the gnawing void that seemed to grow with every new triumph.

He pushed his chair back, standing up slowly. The room was silent now, save for the distant murmurs of celebration. He had everything a man could want: wealth, power, respect. Yet, when the initial joy wore off, it felt like a puzzle he couldn't quite piece together.

"Everything is always temporary," he muttered under his breath, turning toward the door. His reflection in the window caught his eye—a man in his mid-forties, impeccably dressed, successful by every measure. But beneath the surface, the weariness in his eyes betrayed a deeper truth. He had built an empire, but he hadn't built a life.

The door swung open, and his assistant, Lila, appeared in the doorway, her bright eyes scanning him with an energy he no longer felt. She smiled. "You don't want to miss the toast. The board's already talking about next quarter's targets."

The words hit him like a hammer to the chest. Targets. Always targets. More to achieve, more to prove. A cycle he couldn't break, even if he wanted to. He had never been able to turn off the pursuit. But lately, the relentless chase felt… futile.

"I'll be down in a moment," he replied, his voice steady but distant. The door clicked shut behind him, and he stood there for a moment longer, staring at the empty glass on his desk. The familiar swirl of champagne, a symbol of fleeting victories, was waiting downstairs, but somehow, it didn't feel as sweet as it once had.

The sound of laughter from below seemed to mock him. In the absence of real connection, he had filled his life with distractions—money, success, status—anything that could momentarily drown out the rising question at the back of his mind.

He was a man of ambition, yes. A man of wealth and power. But was he truly a man of happiness?

## The Unfamiliar Dawn

Ryan's head throbbed, a dull, persistent ache that matched the disorientation sweeping through him. His eyelids fluttered open, but everything around him was a blur. He blinked a few times, squinting against the soft, diffused light streaming through the small window. The first thing he noticed was the smell—fresh, earthy, like the scent of wood and grass, untainted by the sterile air of his office or the clean, artificial scent of the luxury hotel suites he'd grown used to.

He groaned as he sat up, running a hand through his disheveled hair. His fingers brushed against something rough—a woolen blanket—and the bed he was lying on was far too simple, too primitive for his accustomed taste. This wasn't his sleek, expensive hotel room. In fact, it wasn't anything he recognized at all.

The room around him was small, almost cramped. Wooden walls, the floor worn with age, a tiny kitchen nook tucked against the far corner. He could hear the faint sound of birds chirping outside, the kind of natural noise that was as foreign to him as the sudden sense of vulnerability coursing through him.

Where was he?

He swung his legs over the side of the bed, his feet meeting the cool wooden floor. The headache from the alcohol hung over him like a thick fog, but something else—a sharper, more pressing feeling—cut through it: confusion. He didn't remember how he got here. He didn't remember anything after the party, really. Just fleeting images of clinking glasses, laughter, and then… nothing.

He stood up, steadying himself against the wall. His head swam for a moment, but he pushed through it, the instinct to understand driving him forward. The door was ajar, and curiosity urged him to step outside.

He pulled it open and stepped out, squinting against the sunlight. The first breath he took was crisp, cool, and smelled of fresh grass. He was... *somewhere*. Somewhere far from the confines of his penthouse and boardrooms. He looked out at what could only be described as a paradise—vast green pastures stretching out before him, with rolling hills dotted with wildflowers. And far beyond, the jagged, snow-capped peaks of mountains standing tall and serene against a bright, endless sky.

He stumbled forward, each step unsteady as he tried to make sense of the scene unfolding around him. This was no place he recognized. No city, no building, no familiar landscape. Just... nature, as if he had been dropped into the heart of it, the world untouched and unspoiled.

He walked aimlessly, his mind racing to find any explanation. How had he ended up here? Had someone drugged him? Was this some kind of joke, some elaborate trick?

Then he saw him. An old man, bent but steady, tending to a cow by a small wooden fence that marked a boundary between the hill and a stream that snaked through the valley. The man was wearing simple clothes, a faded tunic and trousers that looked as though they had been mended many times. His hands, though rough with age, moved with care as he adjusted the cow's tether.

Ryan's steps faltered. There was something calming about the old man's presence, a quietness that contrasted sharply with the frantic energy of his own mind. But before Ryan could call out, the man's voice broke the silence.

"Good morning, Ryan. Did you sleep well?"

The words hit him like a wave. He froze, his mouth drying instantly. How did he know my name?

The old man looked up, catching Ryan's wide-eyed gaze. A soft, knowing smile spread across his weathered face. He spoke again, his voice gravelly but kind. "You must be wondering where you are."

Ryan opened his mouth to speak but found himself unable to form words. The questions piled up, each one more urgent than the last. He opened his mouth again. "Where am I? How did I get here?"

The old man nodded slowly, his smile never wavering. "You are here, Ryan. This is the place where people long to be when they've spent a lifetime chasing the noise. But few find their way, and even fewer stay. The world is full of distractions, you see. People are always too busy, too loud. They never pause long enough to notice the silence, the peace that lies just beyond the chaos."

Ryan's confusion deepened, a frenzied pulse of frustration rising within him. "This doesn't make sense," he muttered, more to himself than to the old man. "I don't belong here. I—I don't even know how I got here. What is this place? Why am I here?"

The old man's eyes glinted with quiet wisdom as he turned back to his cow, securing its tether. He took a deep breath and sighed as if listening to something in the distance only he could hear. "This is the place that calls to those who have become weary of the noise. You may not understand now, but in time, you will. It's a place where one can finally hear themselves again, beyond all the distractions."

Before Ryan could reply, the old man began to walk slowly toward the stream, his steps deliberate and steady, as though he were unhurried by time. He didn't wait for Ryan to follow, but it was clear that he was expected to.

Ryan stood still for a moment, his mind scrambling to make sense of it all. The old man's words echoed in his mind, a confusing riddle. The noise. The distractions. The silence.

Unable to make sense of it, but unable to resist the pull, Ryan followed, his feet moving on their own as he trailed behind the old man.

He could feel the weight of his own thoughts bearing down on him, a thousand questions circling in his mind, but no answers in sight.

And yet, for the first time in years, there was a strange peace in the air - an almost tangible quiet that seemed to settle into his bones.

## The Stream of Silence

The grass beneath Ryan's feet was cool and soft, the earth clinging to his shoes with each step. The old man's pace was slow, deliberate, and Ryan found himself following without really thinking. The air was crisp, the kind of freshness that felt cleansing with each breath. The scenery around him—a perfect landscape untouched by time— seemed surreal. The gentle sway of the grass, the distant sound of the stream, and the soft chirp of birds made him feel as if he had stepped into another world entirely.

As they approached the stream, its clear waters shimmered under the early morning light. The stream was small, but it flowed with a tranquil persistence, its path winding lazily through the valley, bordered by smooth stones and lush greenery. The sound of the water was calming, almost hypnotic, as it tumbled over the rocks in a quiet symphony of nature.

The old man paused at the water's edge, lowering himself carefully to a large rock beside the stream. He sat with ease, the years of age evident in the careful way he settled, his back straight even with the weight of time. He didn't look at Ryan, but instead let the silence settle between them, as though he were waiting for something.

Ryan stood for a moment, still uneasy, his mind racing with thoughts that refused to form into clear questions. The beauty around him made it even harder to understand why he was here. This isn't real. This can't be happening.

Finally, he couldn't stay quiet any longer. His voice came out sharp, almost frantic, breaking the stillness of the morning. "What is this place?" he asked again, more insistent this time. "And why am I here? What do you want from me?"

The old man looked up at him, his expression soft but knowing. He didn't seem alarmed by the urgency in Ryan's tone. Instead, he simply regarded him with quiet understanding, as though he had been expecting these questions.

"This is the place where people come when they've had enough," the old man said slowly, his voice steady, as if he were explaining something as natural as the rising sun. "When they've reached the end of the road they've been on for so long and finally realize that they've been chasing the wrong thing. Here, there is no more noise, no more distractions. Just you and what you need to hear."

Ryan's heart skipped a beat. His throat tightened as the words settled in, and for a moment, he felt something stir within him—an uncomfortable recognition. It was as though the old man was speaking directly to the core of what Ryan had been feeling for so long but had never been able to articulate.

"No more noise?" Ryan repeated, the words feeling foreign on his tongue. "What are you talking about? My life... it's not about noise. It's about—about success. I built everything I have."

The old man's smile was gentle, almost pitying, as he nodded slowly. "Success is an idea, not a place. And you've worked hard for it, I'm sure. But it's not enough, is it? You feel it now, don't you?"

The words hit Ryan harder than he expected, a flicker of something cold and unsettling washing over him. He opened his mouth to argue, but the words felt stuck in his throat. He thought about the countless hours spent in meetings, the endless deals, the late nights at the office, the constant push to do more, to be more. All of it now seemed so distant, so trivial.

He turned his eyes to the stream, watching the water flow with quiet determination, never wavering from its path.

For the first time, he noticed the way it moved—calmly, steadily, without urgency. It had no destination to rush toward, no goal to meet. It just was.

And suddenly, the weight of his own life, his business, his never-ending chase for more, felt suffocating. He inhaled deeply, but the air didn't seem to fill his lungs as it should. It felt shallow, like he was trying to breathe in something that wasn't meant for him.

"Why does it feel like I'm suffocating?" he muttered, more to himself than to the old man.

The old man's gaze softened. He said nothing, but his silence spoke volumes.

Ryan stepped forward, unconsciously moving toward the stream. His shoes sank slightly into the soft earth as he knelt down beside it, his fingers grazing the surface of the water. The coolness sent a shiver down his spine. He felt the pull of the place, the serenity of it, and yet it only deepened his confusion. How could something so peaceful feel so foreign? How could something so simple be so difficult to understand?

"You've spent your whole life chasing what doesn't last, Ryan," the old man said quietly, his words weaving through the air like the stream. "You've built an empire, but what you've never built is peace."

Ryan's jaw tightened. His eyes narrowed, and for a moment, frustration flared in his chest. "I don't need your philosophy," he snapped, his voice rising. "I don't need to be lectured by some—some old man in the middle of nowhere!"

The old man didn't flinch. His eyes remained calm, and he simply nodded, as though he had been expecting this reaction.

"Of course you don't," he said. "But you will. The question is not whether you want peace. The question is whether you can allow yourself to find it."

Ryan stood up abruptly, his breath quickening, and for a moment, he felt like a stranger in his own skin. This place, this quiet, this man—it was too much. Too unfamiliar. His whole life had been built on achievements and noise, on the rush of success, on the validation of others. And now, here he was, standing beside a stream, feeling more lost than he ever had.

Without another word, he turned and began walking back, his steps hurried. The old man didn't stop him, nor did he call out. He simply watched as Ryan retreated into the distance, the sound of the stream still whispering in the background.

## The Calm Within

Ryan hadn't made it far. He had only walked a few paces before something stopped him—something quiet but powerful.

It wasn't just the gentle rush of the stream or the peaceful hum of the world around him. It was a feeling that rose within his chest, warm and unfamiliar. It was sudden clarity that rushed in like sunlight breaking through a storm.

He could breathe. And it wasn't the shallow breaths he was used to – the tight, anxious breaths that came with meetings, deadlines, expectations. No. This was full, deep breathing. The kind of breath that didn't feel like a burden. The kind of breath that let him feel lighter, almost as if the weight of his years of worry had lifted, if only for a moment.

For the first time in so long, he felt like he could hear everything clearly. The rustle of the wind, the soft gurgling of the stream, the chirping of the birds in the trees. And then… there was something else. Something he hadn't noticed in his previous life: *magic.*

It wasn't something he could explain in words, but he could feel it in his bones. The world around him—this place, this moment—felt *alive* in a way he hadn't imagined. It was as if he had only been half-living all these years, chasing something so fleeting, so illusory. But now, here, in this quiet space, he felt something true. Something enduring.

For the first time, he understood the difference between pleasure and peace.

He inhaled deeply, and as he did, the cool, fresh air seemed to sweep away the layers of anxiety, worries, and loneliness that had built up over the years. The heaviness he had carried with him—always chasing the next achievement, the next target—was gone. He felt lighter, freer, as if his soul had been unburdened by the very thing that had been weighing it down all this time.

Ryan stood still for a moment longer, letting it all wash over him. There was a quiet joy in this simple moment. A quiet joy he'd never experienced, despite all his wealth, despite all his success.

Without thinking, he turned back toward the old man. The decision felt natural. As if he had no choice but to return, to sit beside the source of the peace he now craved.

The old man was still seated on the rock, his eyes fixed on the stream, unmoved by Ryan's approach. Ryan, a man who had always been in constant motion, suddenly found himself longing for stillness.

He sat down beside the old man, his legs folding beneath him, the ground beneath him solid and grounding. He felt the coolness of the rock against his palm, and for the first time, he wasn't distracted by it. His mind was clearer, and the weight in his chest was gone.

"I don't know where I am," Ryan said, his voice quieter than before, softer, as though speaking too loudly might shatter the calm. "But I feel… good. I feel more… *alive* than I have in years."

The old man turned his gaze to Ryan, a knowing look in his eyes. It was as though he had been waiting for this moment all along.

"You feel it now, don't you?" the old man said softly. "The peace. The stillness."

Ryan nodded, his throat tight. He couldn't find the words to express the shift inside him, but he knew it had happened. A part of him that had been hollow for so long was filled, not with more things, not with more success, but with something intangible. Something that didn't need to be earned or chased.

The old man's voice broke the silence again, gentle but firm.

"You spent your life pursuing what you thought would make you happy, Ryan. You believed that wealth, power, and position would give you the happiness you sought. And for a time, they did. But only for a short while. You got pleasure—fleeting, temporary pleasure. But it was never true happiness."

Ryan shifted, discomfort curling in his chest. The old man's words pierced through the carefully built walls around him. He had spent so long thinking that the next achievement, the next big deal, would be the one to fill the emptiness inside him. But it never did.

"That's exactly what it was," Ryan muttered, the weight of his realization sinking in. "Pleasure. But it always faded. I always had to chase the next thing. And even when I got it, it felt… hollow."

The old man nodded, his expression never changing. "That's the trap. The cycle. You keep chasing after what you think will give you joy, but all you're doing is running away from the very thing you need. *You* were always what you needed, Ryan. But you were too busy, too distracted to see it."

A silence fell over them both. The only sound was the steady flow of the stream, the rustling of the leaves, and the soft breath of the earth around them.

"And now?" Ryan asked, his voice quieter, as if he were testing the waters of this new reality. "What do I do now?"

The old man's gaze softened, a slight smile tugging at the corners of his lips. "Now, you learn to see the world differently. You stop chasing. You stop trying to fill a void that was never there to begin with. You open your eyes to the beauty of life as it is—no more, no less. Every day is an opportunity to see goodness, hear magic, and feel peace. It's all around you, if you're willing to pause and let it in."

Ryan looked down at the stream again, watching the water flow effortlessly past him, a simple, natural rhythm that never sought approval or validation. He closed his eyes for a moment, letting the words settle within him.

For the first time in years, he felt no pressure, no expectation. No *need* to prove anything.

He wasn't sure where he was or how long he would stay, but in that moment, it didn't matter. The world had slowed, and for the first time in a long time, Ryan was finally still.

## The Return

The sun had risen higher in the sky, casting a golden light over the pasture. Ryan sat there, his legs crossed beneath him, his back straight as he breathed deeply, absorbing the cool breeze that swept over the valley. It was more than just a breath of air—it was life itself. He felt it as it passed through him, the coolness swirling around his body and clearing his mind. For the first time, he wasn't rushing to go somewhere or achieve something. He was simply *being*.

He marveled at the way the grass swayed gently in the wind, the way the flowers bloomed in delicate, vibrant colors that he had never fully noticed before. Deep purples, bright yellows, fiery reds. Each petal was like a small miracle, a stroke of life that he had overlooked in his quest for more. Butterflies floated lazily from one blossom to another, their wings flickering in the sunlight like delicate pieces of silk.

A smile tugged at the corners of his mouth. It was a smile he hadn't worn in years – a smile that came without effort, a smile that didn't require anything to be perfect or accomplished. It was simply the smile of someone who had noticed *something beautiful* for the first time in a long while.

The old man stood beside him, watching the scene unfold. There was no judgment in his gaze, only quiet satisfaction.

"You're seeing it now, aren't you?" the old man said, his voice soft but knowing. "The beauty that was always here. You've begun to slow down and really see life for what it is."

Ryan nodded, the words sinking deep into him. It was as though a veil had been lifted from his eyes. The world had always been full of wonder, full of magic, but he had been too busy to notice. The simple act of breathing, the gentle wind, the colors of the flowers— all of it had always been there, waiting for him to stop and appreciate it.

But then, the old man said something that struck Ryan to the core.

"This green pasture," the old man continued, his voice low, "is not just the beauty of the world around you. It's your own deep inner mind. This place, this peace, has always been inside you. But it's been hidden beneath the noise, beneath the distractions of your life. And so, you've forgotten what true happiness feels like."

Ryan froze. The old man's words were like a ripple through a calm pond, unsettling everything he thought he knew.

"Wait, what do you mean?" Ryan asked, his voice quiet but full of confusion. "This—this pasture? My mind?"

The old man smiled gently. "Yes. The very thing you've been chasing all your life—happiness—has been right here all along. But you couldn't see it because you didn't slow down enough to look. The pursuit of success, wealth, and external validation made you forget what was inside. You've grown weary, tired, like the folds of my face. And now, this beautiful place, this tranquility, is the reflection of the peace within you—waiting for you to remember."

The words hung in the air, thick with truth. Ryan sat in stunned silence, trying to make sense of what the old man was saying. His entire life had been a chase for happiness, a chase that led him to empty victories and fleeting moments of joy. But now, it was as though everything had come to a halt, as if he were looking into a mirror for the first time and seeing his true self—not the man he had built, but the person who had been buried underneath the weight of his own ambition.

The realization hit him like a wave, washing over him and leaving him breathless. He didn't need to search for happiness in the distant horizons of success, in the stacks of money, or the constant striving for more. It was always there, within him, waiting for him to stop and breathe. He had just never taken the time to feel it.

Suddenly, without realizing it, Ryan closed his eyes. A single tear escaped from the corner of his eye and fell down his cheek. The floodgates opened, and tears began to flow freely, each one carrying the weight of years of frustration, confusion, and loneliness. But now, there was a sense of relief in it, a release.

He wasn't crying out of sadness; he was crying out of *understanding*. He had been looking in the wrong place for so long. And now, at last, he was awake.

The sound of a soft knock broke through the silence. Ryan's eyes snapped open, and the peaceful world of the pasture began to dissolve around him. The stream, the flowers, the old man—everything faded away like mist evaporating with the dawn.

He blinked, disoriented. He was no longer on the hillside. He was back in his room—his own familiar bedroom. The walls, the furniture, the familiar scent of his home— it was all there. He rubbed his eyes, not sure if he had been dreaming or if everything he had just experienced had been real.

Another knock.

"Ryan? Are you awake?" The voice on the other side of the door was familiar, soft, and full of love. His wife.

His heart pounded in his chest as he stood up slowly, his hands shaking. He walked toward the door, his mind still clouded with the echoes of what he had just felt—the peace, the clarity, the magic of the world around him.

He opened the door, and there they were – his wife, his children. Standing in front of him, smiling with concern and affection, as if nothing had changed. But everything had changed.

For a long moment, Ryan simply stood there, frozen in place. He looked at the faces of his wife and children, their warmth, their love. He saw the innocence in their eyes, the joy that filled the room just by their presence.

And in that moment, he knew—*he was different.*

With no words, he stepped forward and wrapped his arms around them, pulling them close. He felt his wife's familiar embrace, the warmth of his children against his chest, and for the first time in years, he didn't feel the weight of worry, of expectations, of the constant chase. He felt *present*. He felt like he was exactly where he was supposed to be.

"I'm here," he whispered, his voice trembling. "I'm finally here."

And with that simple truth, Ryan understood that happiness wasn't something to be chased. It was something to be *lived*.

And for the first time, he was ready to live it.